Managing and Employing People

THOROGOOD

THE PUBLISHING
BUSINESS OF THE
HAWKSMERE GROUP

**Published by Thorogood Limited
12-18 Grosvenor Gardens
London SW1W 0DH.**

**Thorogood Limited is part of the
Hawksmere Group of Companies.**

© Project North East 1998

All rights reserved. No part of this publication may be reproduced, stored in a retrieval system or transmitted in any form or by any means, electronic, photocopying, recording or otherwise, without the prior permission of the publisher.

This Pocketbook is sold subject to the condition that it shall not, by way of trade or otherwise, be lent, re-sold, hired out or otherwise circulated without the publisher's prior consent in any form of binding or cover other than in which it is published and without a similar condition including this condition being imposed upon the subsequent purchaser.

No responsibility for loss occasioned to any person acting or refraining from action as a result of any material in this publication can be accepted by the author or publisher.

A CIP catalogue record for this Pocketbook is available from the British Library.

ISBN 1 85418 074 6

Printed in Great Britain by Ashford Colour Press.

Designed and typeset by Paul Wallis at Thorogood.

Front cover: © Bridgeman Art Library
– *The Rehearsal of the Ballet on Stage* by Edgar Degas.

Business Action Pocketbooks

Business Action Pocketbooks are concise but comprehensive reference books designed to fit in your pocket or briefcase to be a ready source of business information. Each *Pocketbook* gives an introductory overview of a single topic and is followed by around 20 sections describing a particular aspect of that topic in more detail.

Pocketbooks will be of use to anyone involved in business. For owner managers and for managers in bigger businesses they will provide an introduction to the topic; for people already familiar with the topic they provide a ready reminder of key requirements. Each section concludes with a checklist of useful tips.

This book is based on *Business Information Factsheets* researched and written by enterprise and economic development agency, Project North East. Section contributors include Linda Jameson, Andrew Maville and Bill Waugh all of whom work at PNE. The series has been edited by David Irwin.

The information is checked by an independent expert to ensure, as far as possible, that it is accurate and up to date. However, neither the publishers nor the authors can accept any responsibility for any actions that you should take based on its contents. If you are in doubt about a proposed course of action, you should seek further professional advice.

Other titles in the 'Pocketbook' series

Business Action Pocketbooks are a series of concise but comprehensive reference books. Each one contains sections describing particular aspects of a topic in detail and checklists with useful tips.

Building Your Business

This *Pocketbook* provides practical information about growth, strategy and business planning. Effective leadership, problem solving, decision making and the formal aspects of running a business are also covered in this guide which will help to define your strategy and ensure that you achieve your stake in the future.

Developing Yourself and Your Staff

Team building, personal development, managing meetings, stimulating staff and quality management are all covered in a clear and practical way for the busy manager in this *Pocketbook*. By developing your people through teamwork, training and empowerment you are developing your business – this book tells you how.

Finance and Profitability

Practical tips and techniques for profitable management, including costing and budgeting, record keeping and using financial statements and understanding and finding investment are covered in this *Pocketbook*. Advice is also given on financial forecasting, monitoring performance against your plans and retaining effective financial control. This book will help ensure that your business is successful and profitable.

Sales and Marketing

This *Pocketbook* is an excellent reference tool focusing on the overall process of sales and marketing. It will help give you a direction and a set of goals along with practical tips and techniques for successful market research, segmentation and planning, promoting, selling and exporting. It will help you take those first important steps towards establishing a presence in your market.

Contents

Introduction

The importance of people 1

PART ONE
Recruiting staff **17**

1. Basic staff planning 19
2. Staff recruitment 29
3. Job descriptions 41
4. Person specification 51
5. Advertising for staff 61
6. Interviewing for staff 73

PART TWO
Employee rights **83**

7. Equal opportunities at work 85
8. Maternity rights 95
9. Employing people with disabilities 107
10. Disability Discrimination Act 1995 117

PART THREE
Employer obligations **129**

11 Contracts and conditions of employment 131

12 Personnel policy statements 141

13 Induction and introduction of new employees 151

14 Salaries and other financial rewards 161

15 Absence and sickness 171

16 Employee relations 181

PART FOUR
Effective management **191**

17 Staff appraisal 193

18 Disciplining staff 203

19 Dismissal 215

20 Redundancy 225

21 Handling conflict between employees 235

PART FIVE
Trade unions and industrial relations **245**

22 Trade unions and the law 247

23 The Trade Union Reform and
   Employment Rights Act 1993 255

24 Transfer of Undertakings (Protection
   of Employment) Regulations 1981 265

PART SIX
Appendices **277**

25 Checklist for first time employers 279

26 Further reading 289

27 Useful addresses 299

Index 305

Introduction

The importance of people

A business depends on the people running it. Effort spent on human relations and people management will be repaid many times over.

There are a number of areas where problems may occur. These will reduce the efficiency of any business. They include:

- Poor recruitment and selection – staff lack the knowledge, personality, or skills necessary for the business.

- Confused organisational structure – the way in which staff are organised is wasteful and inefficient.

- Inadequate control – poor decisions are made because of faulty information (possibly in the hands of inappropriate people).

- Poor training – staff have not been taught skills which could significantly improve their job performance.

- Low motivation – staff are not concerned about the business and will not spend much effort to further common goals.

- Low creativity – good ideas for improvement are not being put to use, so stagnation occurs.

- Poor teamwork – staff do not work together, or find that there are too many obstacles to working together.

- Lack of succession planning and management development – sufficient preparation for important future job vacancies is not being undertaken.

- Unclear aims – the reasons for doing things are either muddy or badly explained.

- Unfair rewards – staff are not rewarded to their satisfaction.

- Unrealistic expectations – you expect too much of your workforce.

- Poor staff planning – having the wrong number of people, either too high or too low, or having people with inappropriate skills and abilities.

Maslow's hierarchy of needs

Abraham Maslow (1954) developed one of the most influential theories of human needs. He started from the point that humans have a variety of needs some of which are more fundamental than others. He noted, for instance, that the need for food was paramount to the hungry but that people who had sufficient food had different needs. Maslow's ideas have had an enormous impact on the thinking of managers and social scientists.

Maslow grouped his needs into five basic categories and arranged them in a hierarchy from higher to lower. In Maslow's view lower needs had to be satisfied at least in part before higher needs could be addressed. Strategies to satisfy lower needs dominate behaviour until they are satisfied when strategies to satisfy higher needs take over.

Maslow's hierarchy of needs

If we accept these ideas it means that an employee's and a manager's behaviour will vary in accordance with the satisfaction of need. It means also that systems designed to motivate – pay, benefits etc must adapt because of the change in the way in which people meet their needs.

In organisational terms, Maslow's theory means that we must constantly upgrade the way in which we manage staff. Pay may be enough to help them satisfy their lower level needs but we may then need to introduce job security to offer safety needs, team working to offer belonging needs, job redesign and authority to offer needs for esteem and training and development to offer needs for self actualisation.

Putting Maslow to work

Frederick Herzberg tried to put Maslow's theories into action. He carried out a number of surveys in which he asked employees to talk about the times when they felt best and worst about their jobs.

The dominant theories in 'good feelings' stories were achievement, recognition for performance, responsibility, advancement and learning. The 'bad feelings' stories were about things such as company policy, administration, supervision and working conditions.

Herzberg called those aspects of work that produced job satisfaction motivators and those that produced job dissatisfaction hygiene factors. Hygiene factors do not motivate if they are improved, but if they fall below a certain level, they become a source of demotivation or dissatisfaction. In effect, Herzberg took Maslow's hierarchy and divided it in two, regarding physiological, safety and belonging needs as hygiene factors and self esteem and self actualisation needs as motivators.

Herzberg's hygiene factors dealt with the environment in which the work was carried out whilst the motivators concerned the work itself. He argued that all the methods used to motivate staff – better pay, better benefits, training etc were variants of what he called the KITA approach to motivation – the belief that the surest and quickest way to get something done was to kick them in the backside. In Herzberg's view KITA approaches do not motivate – they may get the person to move but not necessarily in the right direction and they will soon need another kick to get them to move again.

Herzberg argued that the idea of job design and enrichment was central to motivation. He saw job enrichment as being the process of 'vertical job loading'. This is done by adding to the job factors which gave employees more autonomy, more freedom, more challenges and more feedback about their performance.

X and Y

Douglas McGregor took Maslow's theory of motivation and added another dimension. McGregor felt that the perspective of the manager would determine their response to work.

McGregor writing in the 1960s suggested that most managers subscribe to what he called Theory X, which suggested that managers need to direct and control subordinates assuming:

- The average human being is pensive and lazy, has an inherent dislike of work, will avoid it if possible and has little ambition.

- Because of this human characteristic of dislike of work, most people must be coerced, controlled, directed and threatened with punishment to get them to put forth adequate effort towards the achievement of organisational objectives.

- The average human being prefers to be directed, wishes to avoid responsibility and wants security above all.

There was a wide variation in Theory X assumptions ranging from the belief that managers need to coerce, threaten, control and punish staff to the thought that a persuasive style will help everyone to get along. This might produce a superficial harmony which in the long run causes apathy and employees who expect more and more while giving less and less or, at the extreme, leads to low productivity, antagonism and sabotage. Theory X tends to create self fulfilling prophecies.

McGregor argued that evidence from the behavioural sciences, though inconclusive, seemed to indicate the need for a new theory – Theory Y, in which the key proposition is that 'the essential task of management is to arrange organisational conditions so that people can achieve their own goals best by directing their efforts towards organisational rewards.' Theory Y assumes:

- The expenditure of physical and mental effort in work is as natural as play or rest.

- External control and the threat of punishment are not the only means of bringing about effort toward organisational objectives. People will exercise self-direction and self-control in the service of objectives to which they are committed.

- Commitment to objectives is a function of the rewards associated with their achievement.

- The average human being learns under proper conditions not only to accept but also to seek responsibility.

- The capacity to exercise a high degree of imagination, ingenuity and creativity in the solution of organisational problems is widely, not narrowly, distributed in the population.

- Under the conditions of modern industrial life the intellectual potential of the average person is only partially utilised.

It is the job of management to ensure that the interests of the organisation and the interests of the staff coincide.

Pay as a motivator

One of the major elements in giving people the things that they can use to meet some of their needs is pay or reward. Clearly, if you pay someone £25,000 a year, you are giving them a powerful tool in reaching a state where some of their needs are met. Pay will enable them to buy food, drink, shelter, even perhaps some social and psychological needs.

It is dangerous, however, to see money as being the sole or even the best motivator for the type of behaviour that you seek. It also is important to ensure that when you pay to help satisfy someone else's needs that you are motivating the right sort of behaviours.

The first of these is the generally accepted maxim of a fair day's pay for a fair day's work. Pay is usually regarded, at best, as only a short term motivator; but it certainly becomes a source of dissatisfaction if it falls below an acceptable level.

You need to ensure that you are paying enough to get the right sort of person for the job. Pay doesn't only impact on motivation, it also effects recruitment. High calibre staff are invariably in short supply. They will know how much they are worth and will expect corresponding rewards. Any reward system will need to be attractive and competitive.

Pay also needs to reflect performance, though you need to be clear about your chosen performance measures. Failure to do so will result in demotivation and a decline in the performance which you value.

The third issue in reward is not only to ensure that you are rewarding the right sort of performance but that there is some equity in reward between people at lower reward levels in an organisation and those at a higher level. Too great a gap between levels of an organisation may also be demotivating.

Pay is part of a reward strategy. A reward strategy is about developing and integrating a whole range of management tactics to ensure that staff perform which might include:

- Ensure that the organisation can recruit the number and quality of staff it needs to meet its performance targets.

- Be cost effective.

- Develop the 'fit' between organisation and people.
- Provide rewards for good performance and incentives for performance improvement.
- Make sure that similar jobs are paid similar rates (this is a legal requirement).
- Make sure that the different character of different jobs is recognised.
- Create flexibility to ensure that the system can accommodate particular needs (for instance if a company needs an 'expert' who would be paid more than the Head of Department).
- Be robust – this is simple to explain, operate and control.

Managers should ensure that:

- Desired performance is rewarded. In the words of the One Minute Manager, catch staff doing things right and praise them for it. Praise is a great motivator. Do not reward undesirable or neutral performance.
- The relationship between performance and reward is clear. Whatever rewards – pay, promotion, the best parking space, a new job title they are offered should be clearly and explicitly linked to performance throughout the whole of your organisation and should be balanced.

Motivating through work design

Apart from reward there are a number of other ways in which you can motivate staff. As we've seen, Herzberg believed that the nature of the job was central to motivating employees. If jobs are narrow, fragmented and restrictive it is possible to redesign work to make them more appealing. Give staff, for example, increased authority and challenge within the job together with more feedback.

Arguably, three factors are necessary to ensure that job design is successful. Staff need:

- To see their work as meaningful and worthwhile.
- To feel personally accountable for the work that they do.
- To receive effective feedback.

A number of job characteristics will contribute to staff motivation and these can be harnessed by managers to motivate staff:

- Provide variety in the job, the tools used, the place where the job is carried out and the people who the employee meets. Provide opportunities for people to do several jobs or to combine jobs or to rotate jobs.

- Give autonomy in the way the task is performed. Give people responsibility for designing their own working systems.

- Give responsibility. Give people responsibility, for example, for quality control.

- Offer challenges and opportunities for growth and development, for achieving one's potential.

- Give the opportunity to interact with others including colleagues, customer, suppliers etc. Form natural work groups or teams.

- Task significance gives meaning to the job. Show people how their work fits into the overall picture. Ensure that every person's work is significant – and tell them of the importance of their work.

- Everyone needs clearly defined objectives and feedback on performance. Establish relationships with customers and suppliers. Ensure that there are effective feedback channels.

Motivation through participation

The worker participation movement is a result of Elton Mayo's work based upon experiments carried out in the Chicago factory of the Hawthorne Electric Company and in other factories in the United States. Working conditions for one group of staff were changed in an effort to improve productivity. To measure the increase, a control group was also monitored. Unexpectedly, the productivity of both groups increased – which was eventually discovered to be because the control group responded to the interest that was being shown in their work. Morale and productivity both rise when staff are able to participate in the improvement process.

This was discovered again in the 1970s when the work of Joseph Juran and W Edwards Deming and quality circles became popular. Quality circles are groups of people from the same work area who meet voluntarily to focus on issues of product quality. These circles are typically initiated by management asking for volunteers and then training them in problem solving techniques and the way in which groups develop and work. Group members are not given pay for their involvement although participation is recognised in other ways – ceremonies, T-shirts, publicity within the organisation etc. The idea is to give a team responsibility for a whole product, service or project and to provide its members with enough autonomy and resources so that they can be responsible for their own output. Teams meet regularly to discuss scheduling, assignments and current problems.

Motivating through targets

Expectancy or need theories concentrate on the links between goal achievement and performance: if you offer employees the methods to meet their needs they will behave in a manner which ensures that their needs continue to be met.

Links between behaviour and goal achievement are not, however, simple. Individuals have different goals and may only achieve them if they feel they have a realistic chance of obtaining them.

Arguably targets can be set to motivate – 'If you sell a 1,000 units by the end of the month, there will be a bonus of £500' – you satisfy the organisation's needs and you will also be satisfying your own needs. But this assumes that the bonus is a motivator. And the targets need to have a realistic chance of success otherwise individuals will either seek other methods of fulfilling their needs or abandon the task.

In motivating staff it helps to remember that motivation is an individual process. People are motivated by different things. This means that the final step is to individualise the motivation process by:

- Finding out what particular outcomes or rewards are valued by each employee.

- Being specific about the behaviours which represent good performance.

- Ensure that the levels of performance which you decide (targets) are realistic.

- Make sure that there is a direct link between targets and rewards ie that performance lead to outcomes. Without a clear link motivating expectancies will not be created.

- Check that there are no conflicting expectancies ie that levels of performance are linked to different outcomes elsewhere.

- Ensure that changes in reward are large enough to influence performance. Trivial rewards will result in trivial changes in performance.

- Make sure the system is fair.

This *Pocketbook* covers many of the key aspects of recruiting and employing staff, with the exception of personal development which is covered in a companion volume *Developing Yourself and Your Staff*.

Recruiting staff

part
one

1 Basic staff planning

Introduction

As businesses grow, more people are required to carry out the work. New skills are required to handle a wider range of business activities and developing technology. New employees must be put in place in good time to meet increased demand. Opportunities to develop, train and promote existing staff must be taken. Future salary and training costs must be built into the cash flow forecast and financial plan. It is important to foresee these requirements and to plan accordingly. This is staff planning.

Staff planning

Staff planning (sometimes referred to as manpower planning) is an important part of the personnel management function. A number of statistical methods have been developed to help managers analyse, predict and plan future staffing requirements. Most of these methods are only useful for very large workforces. This section looks at the main issues from the point of view of the small business. Each business is different; there is no one best way to plan. The basic approach is as follows:

i) Forecasting sales and planning future production levels.

ii) Estimating the amount and type of work that will be required.

iii) Identifying who can do this work and how training and recruitment can fill the gaps.

iv) Implementing the plan and reviewing its success.

Staff planning is linked to the wider strategic planning process. The staffing plan will develop from the long term forecast for the development of sales and the required increase in working capacity that this represents. The various types of work must be identified and quantified. Costs may then be attached, enabling budgets and finance to be planned. Plans will be required for the long term (eg five years), the year ahead (relating to the annual budget), and possibly a month by month plan showing how change may be phased in during the year ahead (coinciding with the cash flow forecast). All this feeds back into the main strategic plan for business development.

Estimating future work requirements

In addition to estimates for future levels of output, information is needed about how work is done, who does it and what the options are for making changes.

Analysing jobs

The first step is to clarify the main job elements and to determine how much work is required to carry them out. Do not make too many assumptions about what people do and how they do it. The staff themselves are more in touch with how things are really done. A minor task may take much longer than you think. Another task may be so boring that it seriously threatens effectiveness and job satisfaction. Whilst a scientific 'work study' can be useful, informal discussion and team meetings are a much more diplomatic way to look at how work is done.

Estimating increased workloads

From sales forecasts you can derive the required level of production from month to month. These estimates then need to be shown in terms of staffing levels. Clearly, the number of workers required will increase in proportion to the volume of work, eg double the work (usually) requires double the workers. It is often helpful to create estimates based on the amount of work required to produce one unit of production (sometimes known as the Workload Method). The work required to produce one unit is split into its constituent parts. Each part is given a time value. These can then be multiplied by the number of units required, giving the total amount of work of each type. Eg:

Types of work	Time/ unit	@ 180/ month	@ 200/ month
Assembly	1.0	180 hrs (24 days)	200 hrs (26.6 days)
Testing	.4	72 hrs (9.6 days)	80 hrs (10.6 days)
Packaging	.2	36 hrs (4.8 days)	40 hrs (5.3 days)

Fluctuations in demand are important in many industries. In some cases you may need to employ some people on a casual basis in order to meet peak demand. Where possible, plan to switch resources or to build up stock in order to even out these fluctuations.

Analysing the workforce

Profile the people

Summarising and collating information about individuals into a single quick reference document can be very helpful; eg what they do,

Recruitment lead times

It is important to make adequate provision for the time it takes for new people to settle in. Even the most competent people take time to learn about the job and to gain the trust of their colleagues. If you do need to recruit, the lead times for advertising, selection, notice periods, training and induction can be long. You may need to start the whole process as much as six months in advance of the time when the person's full workload will be required. Recruitment is also a significant workload for managers, and this should also be accounted for in your forward planning.

USEFUL TIPS

- *Use simple analysis and planning methods.*
- *Consult with staff about how jobs, individuals and teams can be developed and improved.*
- *Aim to develop and retain your existing workforce.*

2 Staff recruitment

Introduction

In managing a small business, hiring the right people is critical to your success. Your staff or 'human resources' can be a valuable asset; they may also constitute your firm's largest overhead cost.

Because of the expense involved in hiring new staff (both in the time spent on the overall selection process and the money spent on advertising the position), you will want the recruitment process to be as quick and efficient as possible, allowing you to interview a pool of qualified applicants and select the most suitable person.

Recruitment

Businesses recruit for several reasons:

i) To carry out new activities

ii) To replace staff who have left

iii) To allow the business to expand.

Whatever your reason, be sure that recruiting is in line with your business strategy and objectives. Consider setting down your ideas in a business plan. Writing things down can help to clarify your thoughts.

Task analysis and job description

Step one in the selection process is to identify the tasks that the employee will need to perform, defining the activities and responsibilities for each. Analyse the tasks to determine the skills, knowledge, qualifications, aptitudes and attitudes required by the person carrying them out.

After analysing the tasks, write a job description. It is an outline of what the job holder must do. It can be given to applicants and will later serve as a written agreement of what is expected.

The job description should be brief but specific about the duties to be performed; it should include:

- Job title
- Supervisor of position
- Purpose of job
- Overall responsibilities
- Main duties for day-to-day work
- Hours required
- Special needs.

Person specification

The person specification is drawn from the task analysis and outlines the skills, knowledge, experience, etc required in a suitable candidate. This can be used as a guideline for designing adverts, assessing applicants, interviewing candidates, and later in appraising the new employee's work.

Avoid setting requirements or standards which no candidate will be able to meet. Consider having a list of minimum criteria and a list of preferred extras. Include:

- Qualifications and experience needed (includes education and training)
- Skills and abilities
- Special interests
- General disposition/motivation
- Special circumstances (includes hours of availability, modes of transport needed, etc).

Alternatives to hiring someone new

After carefully reviewing the task and the person specification, you can decide whether or not you need a new full-time employee to carry out the tasks required. Consider the following options:

Redistribute tasks to your existing workforce

Can the tasks of the job be shared among your current staff? Will it over burden them? It may mean taking time from current projects or involve paying overtime.

Transfer staff or promote internally

An existing employee already knows your firm and will need less training. You already know the employee's working style, dedication, flexibility, strengths, and weaknesses. However, you may be overlooking strong candidates in favour of existing employees who are less well suited. It could also affect staff morale if one person is chosen over another.

Use subcontractors

You could hire an outside business or expert to undertake the tasks. This works best if the job is on a project-by-project basis. Subcontractors can be expensive and you may have less control over the project.

Hire part-time or temporary staff

Part-timers may cost less than full-time staff, but they often need the same training. The main benefit is increased flexibility. Temporary staff contracts should clearly state start and finish dates, extensions, and the likelihood of the post being made permanent. The length of employment for temporary employment must be less than two years.

Job sharing

Two or more employees can take on the tasks of one job. This gives greater flexibility and provides cover when one of the employees is absent or on leave. The workload needs careful consideration and employment costs may be higher.

Advertising and recruitment sources

Your advert and choice of media or recruitment sources should be aimed at the type of candidate you want to reach. The recruitment sources to consider include:

Job Centres

Job Centres provide a free service to employers and active job seekers. Besides referring potential candidates to you, they can give free advice and information on employment issues such as training and legal matters. Many also provide rooms for interviewing candidates free of charge.

Job Centre adverts are seen primarily by active job seekers. Existing job holders who may be well qualified for the position will not see your advert. Job Centres are generally not selective in their referrals. When giving your local Job Centre information on the position available, be sure to provide specific details of your requirements to eliminate the number of unqualified candidates who could be referred to you.

Job Clubs

There may be a Job Club or Executive Job Club in your area (ask your local Employment Service office). Their members are active job seekers (Executive Job Clubs include redundant managers and unemployed graduates). The clubs will usually attempt to find someone close to your specification.

Employment agencies

Employment agencies are generally selective about their referrals. They are the most expensive option, but also offer services such as help in drawing up specifications and adverts. The fee is often negotiable but expect to pay 10 to 20% of the salary of the person you hire.

Universities/local colleges

Local colleges and universities provide a good source of applicants if the position does not require much experience. Most of the applicants will be recent graduates, but you can also find current students looking for short-term work during holidays or on course placements.

Means of selecting candidates for interviews

Depending on how you advertise the position, you may receive a lot of responses. You need an effective way to sift through to find the candidates who are suitable for interview. Three effective ways are:

Application forms

Application forms can be a quick and efficient way to check for basic requirements and compare applicants' qualifications. The drawback is the time it takes to draw one up. The form should ask questions which will allow you to select the most suitable candidate. Bear in mind to:

a) Keep it as short as possible, only ask for information relevant to the vacancy

b) Leave enough room for applicants to answer each question completely

c) Avoid questions about nationality, marital status, age, or dependents

d) Request names of at least two referees, noting that they will be contacted only with the applicant's permission.

CVs

Asking applicants to submit a CV is quick and obtains the details about a candidate's qualifications in a brief, concise order. The overall presentation of the CV can give you some idea about the candidate's sense of style in his or her self-presentation.

Telephone interviews

A telephone interview lets you quickly assess an applicant and convey basic facts about the position and the business to the candidate. If you use this technique to sift quickly through applicants, prepare a list of questions to ask each applicant so that responses can be fairly compared. Keep in mind that:

a) Asking for interested candidates to phone can mean that more people will apply.

b) It is hard to make a fair assessment on the telephone because it only presents a partial impression of the candidate. Be careful not to make too quick a judgement on a marginal candidate.

c) Because you will have to respond to phone calls at all hours, you may not have time to deal with other current business matters.

Interviewing

The process of interviewing is covered in section six, 'Interviewing for staff'.

Offering the position

Once you have interviewed the most qualified candidates and decided upon the most suitable one, make a verbal offer (subject to suitable references) to the candidate and, if accepted, follow it with a written offer detailing:

- Business name and location
- Job title
- Direct supervisor
- Start date
- Salary and when paid
- Hours including overtime, breaks and holiday entitlement
- Benefits, etc
- Trial or probationary period (used as a safety net to ensure the correct decision has been made).

Once the offer is accepted and the references have been checked, you will need to send a letter of rejection to the other interviewees. The letter should be pleasant and offer a brief explanation of why the candidate was not selected. Keep all application forms and letters of rejection on file for three months after making your decision – they may be needed to answer queries from unsuccessful applicants or as evidence if you are accused of discrimination.

Legal aspects of employment

An employer needs to keep up to date on the legislation which protects the rights of both applicants and employees. Job applicants cannot be discriminated against on the grounds of race or sex. Applicants who feel they have been discriminated against have the right to apply to an industrial tribunal for compensation.

Once you begin hiring employees, you must inform your local authority. A job description must be provided to people who will be employed for over 16 hours per week. A statement of the employee's pay must also be provided, showing gross amount, variable deductions, fixed deductions and net pay. If any part of an employee's contract changes, the employee must be informed within a month of the change. A change can only be made with the consent of the employee.

USEFUL TIPS

- *A great deal of legislation applies to employing people. Your local Job Centre or Employment Service office can provide further information on this and other employment issues.*

- *If candidates are expected to have particular skills (eg typing or bookkeeping) it is worth arranging a suitable short test for before or after the interview itself. Let the candidate know in advance that a test will be held.*

- *Make sure that you really do need to recruit.*

- *Remember that your aim is to get the right person for the job, don't just hire someone who shares your interests.*

3 Job descriptions

Introduction

The development of accurate job descriptions can make an important contribution to the effective management and development of the workforce. The end product or service produced by a business is the sum total of all the tasks of all the individuals in the business. If these tasks are not accurately understood (and adjusted as things change) then the manager will not be able to assess how effectively their employees are working and will not be sufficiently aware when there is a need for new skills and expertise to be introduced to the business. Accurate job descriptions are essential because they are the foundation upon which almost all other processes relating to the job are based.

The limitations should also be appreciated. The small business environment calls for a great deal of flexibility from employees. Job descriptions which do not allow for this can become a source of conflict. In some circumstances (eg where the person has wide ranging responsibilities and works closely with the director) a very general description may be appropriate with the emphasis on responsibility and innovation rather than specific tasks.

Definition

A job description is a concise, factual statement (preferably on one side of paper) of the duties, responsibilities, and requirements that must be met for a particular job. It is important not to confuse the job description with the 'person specification'. A job description defines the job itself. The person specification identifies the characteristics necessary to carry out the job effectively. The person specification is derived from the job description so it is essential that the job description is complete and accurate.

Having said this, it must be acknowledged that it can be more convenient to combine the various aspects of the job into one document known as the 'job description', eg with separate sections on The Company, The Job and The Person. For the purposes of this section we look only at 'The Job'.

Uses for the job description

The job description is a basic information tool for both employer and employee. It has a host of uses as a document in itself, and is the starting point for many aspects of the personnel function. Uses for the job description include:

i) Fulfilling the legal requirement to provide new employees with written particulars of terms of employment within two months of their starting work. This should include a basic job description.

ii) Job descriptions enable employers to be familiar with the main functions of the various jobs that allow them to produce their product or service. This is important information for reviewing the overall allocation of human resources, working practices, company training needs, etc.

iii) On a day to day basis it is a useful management tool. It enables employers to assess what can be reasonably required from an employee and how to measure whether work is being carried out effectively. It is a basic reference document for the employee and the employer about the requirements of the job.

iv) The job description is an important reference point for preparing and conducting staff appraisals. You cannot accurately assess the performance of an individual without an accurate definition of what you are expecting them to do in their job.

v) It is very difficult to recruit appropriate new staff without a job description. It provides the basis for the personnel specification by which to short-list and interview job applicants. It should be used to ensure that the job advertisement contains all the relevant facts. It can be supplied to prospective employees (eg those who get in touch when they see the advertisement) allowing them to decide if they can do the job and to prepare information for interview.

vi) It can provide a basis to deal with disputes between employee and employer. The description should define exactly what you are expecting from the employee, so it can be used (and changed) to clear up any misunderstandings. More often, however, the job description can be used as a stick with which to beat the employer if working relations are breaking down. For this reason it is important to have a suitable get-out clause to reduce the risk of the person working to rule. The job description should not be seen as a 'programme' for the person to follow slavishly. If you cannot sit down with an employee and reasonably discuss their duties you have more fundamental human relations problems which need to be addressed separately.

Reviewing the job

When developing the job description it is essential to use only accurate and relevant information. A variety of different methods may be used to gather the information. The choice of methods will depend on the type of job involved, any financial and time limitations that must be considered, and the circumstances under which the information is to be gathered.

The different methods for assembling information include: questionnaires, activity sampling, diary sheets, observation, and interviews. Always use more than one source to gather information in order to help ensure its accuracy. If your business has achieved Quality Standard certification (eg ISO 9000), procedures in the organisation may be documented indicating where responsibilities lie. This will be your main source of information.

It is important to talk to current job holders and managers during the development of the job description in order to use their knowledge of the job. It is also important to present them with the finished document for an inspection of its completeness and validity.

Contents of a job description

i) Job title. Preferably this should indicate the function and the level of the job. Do not give people with modest duties grandiose titles.

ii) Position. The job title of the manager or supervisor to whom the job holder is responsible should be given. The job titles of all those reporting directly to the job holder should also be given.

iii) Areas of responsibility. This section should provide an overview of what the job entails. It should describe as concisely as possible the overall purpose of the job without trying to describe the actual activities carried out. This section should clearly distinguish the job from others and should establish the principal role the job holder is to play, in particular defining the contribution expected in helping achieve the objectives of the company and of their own unit.

iv) Main tasks. There are certain steps required to define main tasks. These are:

   a) Identify and list required tasks. Indicate the objective or purpose of each task but do not describe how it is carried out.

b) Analyse the initial list of tasks and simplify it as much as possible by grouping together related tasks. Try to have a maximum limit of approximately eight main activity areas.

c) Determine the order in which to describe tasks. There are various ways to determine the order to use: frequency with which they occur (hourly, daily, weekly, continually, monthly), chronological order, order of importance, the main processes of management carried out (setting objectives, organising, planning, motivating, etc).

d) Describe each main task separately. Use short numbered paragraphs with no more than two sentences for the description. If necessary, any separate tasks carried out within the task should be tabulated and described under the main task.

e) Give details and examples of quantitative measures of the amount of work involved along with the frequency with which work is carried out and, when possible, the proportion of time involved for a task.

f) Use descriptive headings to group together related tasks. Examples include headings such as 'organising' or 'planning'.

 This section usually also includes a 'catch-all' phrase such as 'In addition the job holder is required to perform other duties assigned by the supervisor /manager from time to time'. This helps ensure that the employee does not unnecessarily try to limit the amount of tasks or responsibilities they would normally accept.

v) Salary, hours and holidays – this should provide information concerning the wage to be paid, the number of hours required, and an explanation of holiday time. This need not always be included on the description document itself. This may be provided to the employee separately (as 'conditions of employment') especially if such terms are subject to negotiation.

vi) Special requirements – this should provide details concerning equipment, tools, or special skills required for the job.

vii) Location of job and any travelling required.

viii) Special circumstances. This includes things such as heavy lifting, unpleasant or dangerous conditions, night shifts, excessive overtime, and considerable weekend working.

ix) Most challenging part of the job. This section can be very useful in helping to attract applicants, it may also be used during the interview process to learn more about the applicant.

USEFUL TIPS

- *If you encounter difficulties formulating a new job description, it may indicate a more fundamental problem. If the role has not been thought through properly you will have difficulty appointing and managing the person. Is there really a job here? Should the duties of others be restructured?*

- *Make regular use of the job description document (eg for the appraisals, reviews, interviews etc). This will increase awareness of its contents, and inconsistencies are more likely to be corrected. Update the job description when there is any change in responsibilities. Do not just look at it when you are recruiting. The employee should have it readily to hand.*

- *Be realistic about what one person can do. Ensure there is space in their working day to rest and to deal with unforeseen problems.*

- *Involve current job holders managers and supervisors in the development of job descriptions.*

- *Use wording that accurately describes the job. For example only say 'engineer' in the job description if in fact the job holder is an engineer.*

4 Person specification

Introduction

It is important to know exactly what you are looking for when you are recruiting a new member of staff. Advertising must be designed to reach the right target audience. Candidates must be selected according to the appropriate criteria. This can be difficult if there are many applications to assess and more than one person involved in selection. A person specification is a very useful tool to help you compare and assess job candidates.

What is a person specification?

A person specification (also known as a personnel specification) is usually written in conjunction with the job description. The job description describes exactly what carrying out a particular job role involves. The person specification is then produced as a profile of the ideal person for that job. It defines the experience, qualifications, and personal characteristics that the job holder needs to possess if they are to carry out the work successfully. It should also include relevant information on any special demands which the job makes on the employee.

Uses and abuses

Recruitment

The job specification is principally a tool to help you carry out the process of assessing job applicants in an efficient and objective manner. Sifting through applications is very time consuming. There is a lot of information to deal with. Applicants and CVs vary and making comparisons can be difficult. A person specification provides a framework for evaluating this mass of information. Many people find it useful to draw up a checklist to score applications under the various categories of the person specification. A similar system can be used to make interview notes. A specification is especially helpful in ensuring that all interviewers are thinking along similar lines.

Other uses

Drafting a person specification ensures that you think through every aspect of the job requirements. This should help you to be more objective about what is involved. Producing a document will help you to keep the key requirements in mind when you advertise, short-list and interview. You can use the document to consult others about the person required and you can keep it on file to save time if and when you have to recruit again. In addition, the document can be referred to when working with staff to assess their performance and to determine any training needs.

Limitations

On the other hand, thinking about the person should not be a paper exercise. There is a danger of overstating the qualifications required for the job. The person may be too narrowly defined, and this may cause you to disregard someone (eg an internal candidate) who could develop into the role (with further training) and may have other useful qualities.

Categories of information

The information that you use to build up your selection criteria may be easier to put together if you can first decide upon a series of category headings under which you can list the desirable qualities. For trained personnel managers, there are two well established methods for categorising the information in a person specification. These are The Alec Rodger Analysis, which uses seven headings, and The Munro Fraser Five Point Plan. Each system has its own supporters, and both have been used successfully. You may wish to look further into these approaches, though they do tend to focus a lot on psychological qualities (especially the Munro Fraser approach which has headings for 'innate abilities', 'motivation' and 'adjustment'), and this can be a tricky area to get into.

It is likely that your categories will be along the following lines:

i) Physical abilities

ii) Qualifications, performance levels and experience achieved

iii) Level of intelligence and common sense

iv) Natural abilities

v) Interests

vi) Personality traits

vii) Personal circumstances.

As an example of how you might fill this in, if the job were for a computer programmer, the list might include:

i) Physical abilities
   - basic keyboard skills

ii) Qualifications, performance levels and experience achieved
   - relevant computing qualification
   - two years experience of programming in a specific computer language

iii) Level of intelligence and common sense
   - able to think logically
   - able to understand complex concepts

Vocational qualifications

Specific qualifications will frequently be required, eg engineering degree, graphic design degree, computing qualifications, etc. On occasions, specific qualifications may be required to operate a particular type of machine. It is important to know what the latest qualifications are.

Experience

A great deal of the necessary level of knowledge and skills can only be attained by experience. For example, methods for managing people can be learned, but the ability to manage can only be tested out by doing it over a period of years. In some jobs, good contacts in the area of business may be very important.

Skills and physical attributes

Where possible, identify the specific skills which the job requires – eg manual dexterity, physical strength and endurance, mathematical skills, languages, writing, planning and time management, social skills, etc.

Personality

Different types of people suit different types of job. A salesperson needs to be very self motivated and independent to survive the trials of life on the road. Some jobs require a meticulous, almost obsessive approach. For others the ability to be flexible and get on with others is essential. A great deal about the person can be deduced from the interests they list on their CV, eg leading positions in clubs, foreign travel, etc. On the whole, the interview is the main opportunity to explore what kind of person you are dealing with.

A useful way to analyse the type of person you are looking for is to list the types of behaviours they would need to show in the course of their work. Imagine the situations in which they will find themselves and how they should behave in order to get the best result. For instance, negotiating industrial contracts requires the ability to press on with proposals and to tolerate disappointments, without losing commitment to producing an end result. Use your analysis to create scenarios in the interview and to explore how the person may handle different situations.

USEFUL TIPS

- *The principle of having a framework to evaluate candidates for a particular job is perhaps more important than the practice. Be flexible and use whatever approach meets your own particular needs.*

iv) Natural abilities
    - good with languages
    - can work alone and in a team
    - can work to tight deadlines
v) Interests
    - sociable
vi) Personality traits
    - confident
    - friendly
    - listens well
vii) Personal circumstances
    - can work extended hours on weekdays and occasional weekends as projects demand
    - willing to travel overseas.

Not all of the areas mentioned will be relevant to every job. The essential thing is to establish some kind of common framework which is meaningful to you.

It is very important not to allow personal prejudices to creep in. A person may have excellent manual skills but present themselves badly. Moreover, there may be a danger of discrimination, eg the assumption that parenthood could affect the ability of a young female applicant to do a job would be discrimination if the same assumption is not made for young male applicants. When drawing up criteria for physical capabilities, you must look at what is realistic for the job if you are to avoid discrimination against people with disabilities.

Drawing up a specification

The sections below discuss the possible characteristics in more detail. Your chosen framework may also be used to draw up a chart to give applicants a rating under each heading.

Academic record

A good academic record does not always mean that a person will be effective in the world of work. Many people who are clearly very intelligent and astute can have poor qualifications. On the other hand, certain jobs require a reasonable level of intelligence, together with the ability to organise and present information within given time-frames. Academic attainments are an important measure of these qualities. For example, a consultant required to analyse problems and to research and present solutions may need to be of 'degree level'. This may be partly due to a need to command the respect of prospective clients.

- *Ensure that the specifications which you lay down for prospective employees are fair and not discriminatory.*
- *Seek tangible evidence from applicants that they can meet the requirements of the job.*

PERSON SPECIFICATION

5 Advertising for staff

Introduction

Advertising for staff can be expensive and time consuming. It is essential to place the right type of advertisement in the right type of media if you are to attract an adequate number of suitable candidates from whom to select your new employee.

Planning the advertisement

Define the job

The job must be precisely defined before you advertise. If you issue a vague description, suitable candidates will be uncertain whether they should apply, and many unsuitable candidates will apply on a speculative basis. It is surprising how often businesses advertise before they have defined what the new recruit is to do. This is bad practice and good candidates will see through it.

Plan ahead

Most businesses need their new staff in place as soon as possible. It is easy to underestimate the work involved, eg developing and agreeing the copy, identifying suitable media, arranging any design. Find out the copy deadlines for the newspaper and allow plenty of time to get everything sorted out. Ensure that someone is prepared to deal with the responses to the advert, whether by phone or post. Ensure the relevant staff are fully briefed and able to cope with any enquiries.

Develop guidelines

If you advertise frequently and if different people are involved each time, it is useful to draw up a guideline. This ensures that your advertisements are consistent and that every factor is covered. It should also streamline the task and save time. The guideline can include artwork for the logo and information about local media. Review quality and quantity of responses in order to ensure that you are doing things properly. If one person is the channel for arranging adverts, this will improve skills and accountability.

Consider an agency

It may be appropriate to use a recruitment agency. This is particularly useful if you are looking for a specialist or a professional where advertising may have to be very specific. This is likely to be costly so be sure to investigate any agency thoroughly. Ask to see a portfolio of their work and clients before you commit yourself.

Contents of the advertisement

The contents of the advertisement will be derived from the job description and the personnel specification Producing these documents will ensure that the job has been analysed at least to some extent. They are also useful to send out to prospective candidates who telephone for further information. A company brochure can also be sent out to give the full picture.

These documents will be the source to provide the following information:

i) Job title.

ii) Responsibilities. The description of the work should be brief and written in such a way that it is meaningful to either a layman or someone suitably qualified. Avoid jargon.

iii) Position. If appropriate, indicate the level of authority in the organisation ie, to whom they will report and for whom they will be responsible.

iv) Business name and activities. You could mention the current status of the company, eg 'fast growing'. It is worth mentioning if the company is well established since people are increasingly concerned about job security. It is important to disclose the location of the workplace.

v) Qualifications required to do the job. Be precise.

vi) Experience required to do the job and the personal qualities necessary.

vii) State the salary and any benefits (or an accurate estimate of them). Adverts that state the salary generate a higher response than others. If you are not prepared to disclose the salary then make no mention of it at all. Job-hunters interpret most ambiguous salary phrases such as 'competitive rates' as meaning low.

viii) Explain how candidates should apply (eg letter, CV, application form or telephone). Name the person to whom the applications should be addressed, do not just state a job title. Include their full address or telephone number. You may also want to suggest that candidates contact you for further details if necessary. Only offer this service if you are prepared to cope with the response.

ix) You may wish to give a closing date. Ideally allow two-three weeks from the appearance of the advert.

Style

The overall style of the advertisement should be informal and friendly. You want to sound approachable. At the same time, stick to the facts and avoid over-chatty comments.

Circulate a draft copy of the advert round relevant people, eg those being replaced or those carrying out the interviews so that any mistakes or misunderstandings are avoided.

Do not hype it up or state the obvious. Do not make claims that you cannot live up to. Do not oversell. Candidates will be suspicious of obviously inflated claims.

Emphasis

Once the contents of the advertisement are established, consider the best way to present the information. Some factors will be more important than others. Think about what the key selling point of the job is and give it emphasis. A boring job might be attractive because it is in a good location, it is well paid, there is scope for promotion or an unusual degree of autonomy, etc.

Emphasise the most important requirements you are looking for from the candidate. This will ensure that the advert attracts the attention of those particularly interested in this aspect. Also be aware of what is likely to put candidates off, eg location. Do not avoid these issues, simply anticipate and try to minimise any objections.

Language

Get your message over briefly and be precise whenever possible. Use simple language and short sentences. This will ensure the candidate quickly understands what the job is about, and can save you money in terms of the space required. A good way to get information across briefly and clearly is to use checklists or bullet points. This is particularly useful for summarising the job description.

Design

Attract attention

The prominence and impact of the advertisement will depend upon how much you are prepared to pay, which depends upon how strongly you wish to promote the job. A large advertisement, a striking design, a bold outline around the advert will make it stand out.

Attract suitable candidates

Flag up the main points candidates are searching for in bold text. Job title is the most important and usually heads up advertisements. Location (if advertising in national media) and salary should also be highlighted. For high level appointments special graphics may be commissioned, but this is best handled by an agency.

Maintain your company image

Any publication concerning your firm has an impact on the image your business projects. You may have a distinctive house style and logo that can be applied consistently to all your advertisements. You can enhance your staff advertising by having a special format designed (including logo, framing, etc) which can be re-used.

Choosing the media

The type of media suitable for your advertisement depends upon the position you are advertising and upon the amount you are prepared to pay.

Understandably the scale of circulation of a newspaper directly affects the cost of the advertisement. Generally it is believed that the quality newspapers are best for advertising managerial, professional and technical jobs. Professional and trade journals are also extremely effective. For most small businesses the usual method of advertising will be through local newspapers.

When you place an advert in a newspaper or journal make sure you provide clear instructions on price, position, layout, etc. Newspaper and journal advertising departments will help in explaining relevant costs, the different types of classification and often provide a design service.

Ensure you select the correct day for your type of advertisement. Many people just buy the appropriate edition for the jobs. Often there is a specific day dedicated to appointments or a designated category of appointments. Be sure to take advantage of any specialist publications which often have a significant following.

Do not overlook other forms of advertising such as Job Centres and Job Clubs. Universities and colleges usually have (free) vacancy lists for graduates. *British Rate and Data (BRAD)* gives details of periodicals and newspapers, their circulation and the cost of advertising. The best market research is to ask people currently working in the field where they would look for a job.

Handling enquiries

Be prepared to cope effectively and efficiently with any enquiries. Speaking to potential candidates over the phone can help the short-listing process. If you intend to do this then have a few questions prepared and ensure the phone is always staffed by suitable, briefed personnel.

If possible, have some relevant literature ready about the position (and the company) which you can send out to interested parties. Be sure to keep all the applications in good order. Hold on to all the responses that you feel are suitable until after the appointment decision has been made. You never know how many people you will need to call in for an interview before a successful applicant is found.

Discrimination

You must use neutral or all-embracing language when referring to marital status, race or gender. For example, refer to 'candidates'; state in the advert that the position is available to both males and females; or, include both gender expressions such as 'steward and stewardess'. There are exceptions to the discrimination laws but they are unlikely to affect small businesses unless the job offered is sensitive to gender (eg a changing room attendant) or race.

'Ageism' is not illegal, although the Department of Employment is endeavouring to encourage employers to eliminate barriers on age. The Institute of Personnel Development produces guidelines on this area which you may find useful. For further information concerning race and sex discrimination see the Sex Discrimination Act 1975 and the Race Relations Act 1976. You can also get advice by contacting the Equal Opportunities Commission who produce a Code of Practice on promoting equality of opportunity and ending discrimination in employment. Most newspapers will also advise you on this.

USEFUL TIPS

- *Find out any relevant copy deadlines and allow plenty of time to produce your advert.*

- *Exercise caution when repeating advertisements in the same medium as diminishing returns quickly set in.*

- *Keep your demands for information from the candidates to the essential minimum. Job-hunters will be deterred if you ask too many questions at this early stage.*

- *Be careful about including personal phrases such as motivation, proven track record, etc. Such phrases are effectively meaningless as most people believe they have these qualities.*

- *Consider advertising expenditure as an investment. You may manage to produce a very impressive short-list of candidates to whom you could refer back in the future.*

6 Interviewing for staff

Introduction

An interview is a meeting between a manager of the business and a candidate who is applying for a job. The meeting is held to assess if there is a correct 'fit' between the available position and the candidate.

While job interviews are generally thought of as a kind of test to determine if a candidate is the right person to suit a particular post, the process works both ways; the candidate will also be assessing whether or not the position suits him or her. The candidate will take into account the tasks involved and the firm's overall objectives, structure and culture.

It is important that you are careful in your choice of the person to interview the candidates. The direct supervisor of the position is not necessarily the best person to conduct the initial interview. A good interviewer must be knowledgeable about the business, its customers, suppliers, objectives, organisational culture, and the qualities the firm is looking for in a candidate. Above all, he or she should be a good communicator; someone who knows how and when to listen as well as how to explain.

The interview is a crucial stage in the recruitment process as it is usually the basis on which a decision to hire or not to hire is made. However, as described in section two, 'Staff recruitment' it is only one of the stages involved in personnel recruitment.

Preparation

From your list of qualified applicants, choose at least five to invite in for initial interviews. Depending on how closely the qualifications of the applicants match the job description, you will want to schedule enough interviews to enable you to eliminate effectively most of the preliminary candidates. However, you will not want to schedule so many that the time taken in interviewing will be an unnecessary cost to your business.

From the first round of interviews, you should have at least two candidates to ask back for a second interview. If your first choice candidate turns down your offer you will have someone to fall back on without having to repeat the entire recruitment process.

Give yourself enough time before each interview to review the candidate's CV or application form and to write down specific questions that you want to ask. Also, briefly list the points you want to cover regarding the business and the position.

Set aside enough time for each interview. Allow about 40 minutes total. This should include enough time for questions from the candidate at the end. If all goes well with the applicant, you will want some extra time to probe further into selected job criteria or the details of a particular experience.

Schedule a break of at least 20 minutes between interviews. You will need this time to make notes of anything said that is not indicated on the CV or application. You will also need some time to collect your thoughts and take a short break. Try not to schedule more than four or five interviews in any one day. After seven or eight interviews, you will not be as fresh for responding to questions asked or to make appropriate decisions concerning a candidate.

Before the first candidate arrives, arrange your interview area. Try to avoid sitting behind a large desk with the applicant seated on the other side. This can intimidate the candidate who may feel inhibited about disclosing important facts or experiences. The best seating arrangement is one in which chairs are set near a small table at a 45 degree angle. They should be spaced at a comfortable distance from each other so that there is ample personal space for both the interviewer and interviewee. Make it clear to fellow staff members that you are not to be interrupted during the interviews.

During the interview

The interview can be broken down into the following stages:

Welcome

Upon the candidate's arrival, put him/her at ease by using selected 'small talk'. Ask if he/she found the location without any trouble, mention the weather, etc. You will want to say something personable so the candidate feels comfortable.

Don't go too far with the small talk, however. Say just enough to form a comfortable transition between the candidate's entrance and the more serious talk about the job requirements.

Supply information

Give relevant background information on the business, including its objectives, organisation, and culture.

Clearly state the tasks involved in the job.

Be clear in stating to whom the candidate will be reporting and the names and titles of staff with whom he/she will be most closely working. If it is a supervisory position, he/she will need to know how many people will be reporting to him/her and their positions.

State clearly the terms of employment including hours, pay, benefits, lunch and breaks, overtime, as well as future opportunities for advancement.

Acquire information

Use open-ended, specific questions about the candidate's background to probe further into his/her experience and qualifications.

If you are not satisfied that the candidate has properly answered your question, it is best to rephrase it rather than simply repeating it. This way, you don't appear to be bullying.

Avoid firing off questions too rapidly.

Focus on topics such as:

a) What the candidate does currently

b) Previous work and education

c) The reason he/she is applying and why he/she would be good in the position

d) Other interests indirectly relevant to the position.

Ask the applicant for questions

An applicant who comes to an interview prepared with well-thought out and well-posed questions most likely has a sincere interest in the post and in your business.

Depending on the level of the position, a good candidate will have researched your firm. You will know how much work went into his/her preparation by the types of questions he/she asks and by how your questions are answered.

Parting

Wrap up the meeting by asking the candidate if he/she has anything further to add.

Explain the next stage in the selection process (eg whether there will be another interview, when the decision will be made (if known), when the candidate will be notified, etc).

Thank the candidate for his/her time.

Do's and don'ts during the interview

i) Represent the job accurately to the candidate. Don't try to glamorise mundane tasks such as filing and form filling. If you present an inaccurate picture, the new employee could decide to leave soon after being hired because his/her expectations were not met.

ii) Ask open-ended questions. Avoid leading questions or those with yes/no answers. Open-ended questions will provide the most appropriate means for the candidate to express him/herself freely in a way that most accurately portrays his/her character.

iii) Control the interview so that time is not wasted on unimportant areas. You may interview some candidates who talk too much on a particular subject out of nervousness or because they are uncomfortable with periods of silence. If this occurs, interrupt politely and move on to the next question.

iv) Cover all terms of employment including salary, benefits, hours, holidays, etc.

v) Be friendly, interested, and neutral.

vi) Don't talk throughout the entire interview. The candidate needs time to tell you why he/she is the right person for the job. Using silence to indicate that it is the candidate's turn to speak gives you just as much control over the interview as you have when you are speaking yourself.

vii) Don't show boredom or impatience by shifting in your seat, shuffling through papers or not answering questions adequately.

viii) Avoid being sidetracked into long discussions on irrelevant topics of shared interest (eg hobbies).

ix) Don't put words into a candidate's mouth by finishing his/her sentences.

x) Don't offer the candidate the job during the first interview. Even if you feel sure that you have found the right person, it is better to wait until the second interview to make an offer. There may be candidates yet to interview who would be even more appropriate for the position. Also, you will want a chance to review the 'pros and cons' before making a final decision.

Post-interview assessment

Immediately after the interview, take time to make notes on anything said that is directly relevant to the decision. Do this while the conversation is still fresh in your mind. The final decision should be based on how closely each candidate matches the person specification for that particular job.

When you have narrowed your selection down to two or three people, ask them for a second interview. Prepare a longer interview this time to give them each a tour of the office and introduce them to some of the staff. At this point you may wish to delve more deeply into what will be expected of them.

USEFUL TIPS

- *There are various questions that you should not ask during an interview. These relate to subjects which may make your selection appear discriminatory on grounds of race, sex, etc. Your local Job Centre or Employment Service office can provide further information on the sort of questions to avoid (as well as on other employment issues).*

- *It is easy to favour an interviewee with whom you identify (eg because of similar interests or background). Always remember that you need the best person for the particular job.*

- *Don't be tempted to make a decision based purely on 'gut feel' or a first impression.*

- *If none of the candidates meets your requirements, it is better to begin the whole process of re-advertising and re-interviewing than it is to choose someone who is not appropriate for the position.*

Employee rights

part two

7 Equal opportunities at work

Introduction

Equal opportunity employment means that every person has the same chance in matters relating to employment. There are four major laws concerned with equal opportunities in Great Britain (there is separate legislation for Northern Ireland, where the Race Relations Act 1976 does not apply). These sets of legislation cover:

i) Race discrimination

ii) Sex discrimination

iii) Equal pay

iv) Disabled workers.

Legislation

i) The Race Relations Act 1976 makes it unlawful to discriminate on the grounds of national origin, colour or race. The act covers:

a) Recruitment

b) Terms and conditions of employment

- c) Promotion, transfer or training of employees
- d) Benefits and services to employees;
- e) Dismissal of or any other detriment to employees
- f) Instructing or pressurising someone to discriminate
- g) Aiding others in discriminating;
- h) Victimisation
- i) Access to training schemes and treatment on or dismissal from these for non-employees.

The Commission for Racial Equality (CRE) publishes a Code of Practice for eliminating racial discrimination. The code is not enforceable by law. It is, however, used in tribunals and must be taken into account if it is relevant to any matter the tribunal has to decide upon.

ii) The Sex Discrimination Acts of 1975 and 1986, and the Employment Act of 1989, make it unlawful for an employer to discriminate against a woman or man on the grounds of sex or marital status. This applies to the same areas as the Race Relations Act, and additionally retirement and dismissal.

viii) Check redundancy, redeployment and retraining criteria to identify any which need to be revised.

ix) Investigate recruitment, training and promotion policies and how they affect full-time and part-time, male and female employees.

x) How are vacancies for entry to your organisation, or promotion or transfer within it, notified? Are members of any ethnic group excluded or disadvantaged by methods currently used?

Guidelines for employers

There are several steps involved in becoming an equal opportunities employer.

i) Formulate a written equal opportunity policy which states your intentions to develop and apply non-discriminatory practices.

ii) The policy should be expressed by, and ultimately be the responsibility of, a senior manager. Commitment by all managers and staff will be necessary.

iii) The policy should be written down and brought to the attention of all employees, Job Centres and recruitment agencies.

iv) Appoint someone to implement, update and monitor the policy. It is best to have a committee to review the policy in action, ie:
   a) Assess the objectives of the policy
   b) Suggest remedies for any failures
   c) Assess the success of remedies.

   Actual staffing will depend on the size of your business but the officer must have full managerial support and authority to be effective.

v) All employees involved in personnel decisions should be given training on the policy and their responsibilities, ie:
   a) Explain forms of discrimination
   b) Educate against prejudices and stereotypes
   c) Stress assessment on the basis of merit and ability.

vi) Examine current practices, policies and procedures on a regular basis. It is important that grievance procedures are set up and employees know about them.

vii) Gather information on the current workforce (ethnic origins and gender) and determine whether you are providing equal opportunities. Also, compare wages to verify differences in pay are based on something other than sex.

viii) Implement a monitoring system which will enable your organisation to:
   a) Make the best use of the talent at its disposal
   b) Reduce staff turnover
   c) Ensure compliance with the CRE's Code of Practice and Race Relations Act
   d) Identify and remove any practice or procedure which could breach either the Sex Discrimination Act or the Equal Pay Act.

ix) Identify and correct discriminations of the past. Positive action steps to take include training members of a particular racial group to help them gain employment in areas where they are under-represented and encouraging members of a particular group to apply for employment in an establishment in which they are under-represented.

USEFUL TIPS

- *As an employer, you should be aware of the enforcement procedures in case a complaint is made against you.*

- *Documenting your equal opportunity steps will give proof of your efforts which can be used if someone makes a complaint against you.*

8 Maternity rights

Introduction

Increasingly women expect to stay at work after having children. More and more children are looked after by nurseries or nannies, and fathers take a greater share of the caring and domestic duties. It is important for employers to be aware of the legislation which protects the employment rights of mothers. It is also important for employers to understand the pressures that new parents, of both sexes, experience.

Maternity rights

i) Under the Maternity (Compulsory Leave) Regulations 1994, women are not allowed to work for their employer for two weeks from the date of childbirth. Employers who allow this can be fined up to £500.

ii) The EU Pregnant Workers Directive was implemented in the UK by the Trade Union Reform and Employment Rights Act 1993 (TURERA). The TURERA 1993 (Commencement No. 3 and Transitional Provisions) Order 1994 activated the start date for the maternity-related aspects of TURERA. These give the pregnant worker, regardless of length of service, certain rights (she retains any further rights she was previously entitled to, eg extended leave):

a) An entitlement to be off work for 14 continuous weeks, or until the birth if this is after the 14 weeks (this is known as 'Basic Leave'). This term can be extended if health and safety considerations prevent her returning. If she is dismissed before the end of 14 weeks, leave ends at the time of dismissal.

b) Paid time off for antenatal examinations.

c) Dismissal can only take place during pregnancy or maternity where there are exceptional circumstances, with no connection to the pregnancy. She is protected from dismissal for four weeks from the end of the 14 weeks if she is unfit to work and has a medical certificate which states this. (This is not an extension of Basic Leave.)

d) Contractual rights and benefits are retained (apart from remuneration) during Maternity Leave.

e) Pay is not less than appropriate sick pay during leave.

iii) Extended Leave is up to 40 weeks, including 29 weeks after the birth. This right is acquired if three criteria are fulfilled:

   a) If the employee exercises her right to basic leave.

   b) If the employee has, by the start of the eleventh week before the Expected Week of Confinement (EWC) been employed by the company continuously for two years, even if she is not necessarily working, eg off sick.

   c) Written notice is given by the employee in accordance with paragraph 3 (ii) below.

Notification of leave

i) To be entitled to Basic Leave a pregnant woman must inform her employer in writing:

   a) That she is pregnant

   b) Of the EWC (or date of birth if this has already happened). If her employer has requested, this must be confirmed with a medical certificate stating EWC from a doctor or midwife, and

   c) Of the date she wants to start her leave. This should be given 21 days before commencement or if not, as soon as reasonably practicable, in writing if requested.

ii) For notification of Extended Leave, the employee must inform her employer, in writing:

   a) That she will be absent because of pregnancy/childbirth
   b) That she intends to return to work
   c) Of the EWC
   d) Of the date she wants to start her leave, which should be given at least 21 days before commencement, or if not, as soon as reasonably practicable.

Commencement of leave

i) Female employees are entitled to take Basic Leave at any time after the start of the 11th week prior to the EWC. Then leave commences through:

   a) The employee giving 21 days notice, or
   b) Childbirth, or
   c) If they are still at work after the sixth week before EWC, absence from work after the sixth week, partly or solely because of pregnancy or childbirth, regardless of notice.

ii) Extended Leave may be started at any point after the start of the eleventh week before the EWC. Childbirth counts as week one; she can return at any point before the end of 29 weeks after the birth if she gives at least 21 days notice.

Return to work

Reinstatement

She has the right to be re-instated with the same employer or its successor, in her old job or an equivalent one, in the same place of work and in the same capacity. If this is not reasonably practical, a suitable alternative must be offered. She retains rights she had, and continuity of service includes leave. Many women seek to return to work on a part-time basis. Although this is not directly the capacity in which she was previously employed, the employee may have a case of indirect sexual discrimination should she be refused a part-time return and either chooses not to return, or returns full-time, but reluctantly. The employer must justify to the tribunal his/her decision that the job must be done by a full-time employee.

Small firms

Firms with five employees or less (including both employees of associate employers and the employee in question) are not obliged to re-employ female employees who have taken Maternity Leave. This right can only be exercised if it is not 'reasonably practicable' for her to return in the capacity she was previously employed or to a suitable alternative form of employment. If the case goes to tribunal, the employer must prove this.

Early return

An employee can return before the end of Basic Leave, but she must give seven days notice of her early return date. If she does not, the employer can postpone her return until notice has been given, but not to a date after the Basic Leave would have expired.

Postponement of return from Basic Leave

Under statutory extension of Basic Leave, an employee may be prohibited from returning to work if a statutory instrument or approved code of practice disallows her working, because she is breastfeeding/has recently given birth. This will continue until the restriction ends. She must be offered alternative work, or if this is not available, receive remuneration whilst suspended.

Postponement of return from extended leave

a) If she has notified a date of return, she can postpone this for up to four weeks by giving her employer a medical certificate before the original notified day, declaring her unfit to work.

b) If she has not notified a date of return, she may postpone return for up to four weeks from the end of 29 weeks from the birth, by submitting a medical certificate.

c) If a work interruption, such as a strike, makes it unreasonable to expect her to come back on the original date, return may be postponed.

d) An employer can postpone the employee's return date for up to four weeks if the employee is informed before the original day of return, and notified of the reasons.

Statutory maternity pay

The Maternity Allowance and Statutory Maternity Pay Regulations 1994 implement the Pregnant Workers Directive with regard to maternity pay. Statutory Maternity Pay (SMP) is claimed back by employers from the government out of their NI payments. The employer can (but is not obliged to) add to this amount. Female employees absent from work are eligible to claim SMP provided they meet certain conditions. SMP is paid at nine-tenths of weekly earnings for the first six weeks, then £52.50 per week for the next 12 weeks. Even if they fail to meet these conditions they may still be eligible to receive a state maternity allowance.

Eligibility

Conditions for employees claiming SMP:

a) They must have served under contractual employment with the organisation for at least 26 weeks ending with the fifteenth week before the EWC. This point is referred to as the Qualifying Week.

b) Absence must be wholly or partly due to pregnancy.

c) They must still be pregnant at the start of the eleventh week before the EWC, or have had the baby at that time.

d) Notification of maternity absence must have been given.

e) The employer must have received evidence of the EWC, normally on form Mat B1 (Maternity Certificate) from their doctor.

f) Their average weekly wage should not be lower than that which qualifies for taxation and payment of National Insurance contributions.

Duration

The length of time over which SMP is payable is referred to as the Maternity Pay Period (MPP), payable over a maximum of 18 weeks. If she is off work for less than 18 weeks, she will only receive SMP for that period. The MPP runs from the eleventh week prior to the date of childbirth at the earliest. If she is off work after the sixth week before EWC with a pregnancy-related illness, the employer can trigger Maternity Leave, and start paying SMP rather than Statutory Sick Pay (SSP).

Administration

92% of SMP can be reclaimed from the Government by the employer, although firms qualifying for Small Employers' Relief (SER) can claim back 100%, plus a percentage of SMP paid to cover secondary NI contributions.

Maternity policy

Employers should have a definite policy to ensure fair treatment of pregnant employees. Female employees, regardless of their circumstances, are often informed of their maternity rights on employment in order to avoid confusion or disagreement at a later date.

Although firms have a basic legal obligation, a number extend their maternity policy to assist pregnant employees further, eg by choosing to pay employees an amount above SMP, extending payment at the higher rate, or allowing paternity leave.

Maternity policies often have a set procedure which covers statutory rights and obligations. There may be a number of additional clauses to an organisation's policy statement. For example pregnant employees may be offered the opportunity to work shorter hours in the period leading up to maternity leave. They may be allowed to work as close to their EWC as they wish, providing standard of work is not affected. If extra contractual maternity rights are given to women, they are allowed to 'composite' their rights, so taking the best bits of their firm's policy, and their legal rights.

An employee wishing to work elsewhere during maternity leave might be permitted to do so provided she requests the company's permission, giving all details of the position (this will effect eligibility for SMP). This is likely to depend on whether it conflicts with the employee's work with the company or is likely to affect her health.

The policy you adopt should be put into words and ought to be included with the conditions of employment you provide to employees. A suitable section might read:

'Statutory Maternity Pay will be payable according to statutory requirements to female staff taking time off for childbirth. Additionally, those staff who qualify for the higher rate of SMP will be paid that rate for the entire 18 week period, provided they undertake to return and subsequently do so.'

USEFUL TIPS

- *When planning your maternity policy, consider the actual needs of your staff rather than the statutory minimum. Needs may vary from job to job and from business to business.*

- *Be prepared to inform staff of their maternity rights and obligations at the appropriate times.*

9 Employing people with disabilities

Introduction

The employment of people with disabilities is something which many people simply do not consider. The subject has, however, received publicity recently because of the Disability Discrimination Act 1995 (DDA) whose measures began to come into force on 2 December 1996 (see section ten 'Disability Discrimination Act 1995'). From that date, all employers have extensive obligations not to discriminate unjustifiably against disabled people.

What is disability?

According to the DDA, a disabled person is anyone with 'a physical or mental impairment which has a substantial and long-term adverse effect upon his ability to carry out normal day-to-day activities'. There are so many different forms and levels of disability that it is difficult to generalise about what people with disabilities can or cannot do.

Legal requirements

Prior to 2 December 1996, the Disabled Persons (Employment) Act 1944 was the legal basis for employment issues facing persons with a disability. Under it, the Disabled Persons' Register and the quota system were established. From 2 December 1996 people no longer register as disabled and the quota scheme ceased to have effect – although employers covered by the scheme at that date must retain quota records until 3 December 1998. People who were registered as disabled with the Employment Service both on 12 January 1995 and 2 December 1996 automatically count as disabled for a further period of three years.

Under the Act, it is unlawful for an employer to discriminate 'for a reason which relates to the disabled person's disability, if he treats him less favourably than he treats or would treat others to whom that reason does or would not apply'. Failure to comply with the new duties could result in the employer being brought before an industrial tribunal. There is no financial maximum on the compensation which can be awarded.

It will not always be illegal to treat someone less favourably because of their disability. Discrimination can be 'justified' if the reason for the adverse treatment is both relevant and 'substantial'.

Employers have a duty to make 'all reasonable adjustments' to buildings, physical features, working arrangements and practices. Adjustments are necessary if the particular disabled person would otherwise be 'at a substantial disadvantage'. It may be that an employer occupies a building under a lease or some other agreement. If a lease prevents reasonable adjustment because it involves changes to the premises, the employer must request permission from the landlord. The landlord cannot unreasonably withhold consent to those changes, but can impose reasonable conditions. If some other agreement – such as a mortgage – prevents a reasonable adjustment being made, it will always be reasonable for the employer to have to try to obtain approval.

The employment section of the DDA affects employers with 20 or more staff. This number is inclusive of permanent staff (full and part-time), temporary workers and workers on contracts. Companies which are employing less than 20 employees are exempt from this part of the DDA but must comply with all other aspects of the Act. Organisations providing supported employment, along with certain charities, may discriminate in favour of disabled people. The new law does not apply to certain groups including fire-fighters and employees working on ships, hovercraft or aircraft.

Employing people with disabilities

According to government figures, a person with a disability is three times more likely to be unemployed than an able-bodied person. Work which is obtained tends to be poorly paid and low skilled. Several organisations aim to highlight the capabilities of persons with a disability and provide practical advice on employing them. Modern technology allows those with a disability to perform on an equal level to able-bodied staff in many areas of employment. Employers often assume that the work on offer is unsuitable for a person with a disability to undertake, but experience has shown that such people are often capable of performing far more tasks than might be expected. Expense and disruption are rarely barriers – a view supported by the fact that smaller firms, with fewer resources, are often more ready to employ a disabled worker. Career advancement is also commonly neglected by employers.

A serious barrier facing persons with a disability is physical access to places of work. Government Access to Work Grants are available to help with the expense of making physical adjustments to buildings. If adaptations are integrated into a general reorganisation of the office they may cause only minor disruption.

Discrimination takes many forms. Blatant prejudice does exist, but subtle, unintentional discrimination is more widespread and must be tackled if changes are to occur. One example of this is when employers ask for abilities which are not actually required to carry out the job, eg requesting a driving licence when driving is not essential. Under the DDA, employers must not discriminate against any disabled person when recruiting. This affects the job specification, application forms, the selection process, the assessment technique(s) and the terms of employment offered. Employees might become disabled or their disability worsen whilst they are in employment. The job content of an employee with a stable impairment might change. Under the DDA, employers must not discriminate against such employees. Possible reasonable adjustments might involve modifying a job to accommodate changed needs, allowing employees time to adjust, eg by allowing them to work at home, or transferring them to a different post within the organisation. Studies have shown that in performance, attitude to work and attendance records, disabled employees are rated as being as good as, or better than, able-bodied workers.

Employment schemes and advisory bodies

Many schemes or advisory bodies provide assistance for persons with a disability and several of these have specific relevance to the prospective, or current, employer. A selection of these are:

i) The Employment Rehabilitation Service run by the Department of Employment assesses the needs and abilities of individuals and proposes a plan of action; this may include a period in a workshop or with a local employer.

ii) Advice and help is available for employers and employees from the Employment Service Disability Employment Adviser, and Placement, Assessment and Counselling Teams (PACTs). They administer the Access to Work and Supported Employment schemes. Employers are encouraged to adopt progressive personnel approaches and officers will visit prospective employers to identify suitable work for persons with a disability.

iii) The Employment Medical Advisory Service advises on the abilities of disabled individuals and their training needs as well as providing down-to-earth guidance on the health pattern of disabilities. Your local EMAS can be contacted through your local Health and Safety Executive.

iv) Under the Supported Employment Scheme an employer provides work for a person with a disability if they are capable of an output at least a third of that of an able-bodied person. The employer pays an allowance to an official sponsor of the registered person who is then responsible for the individual's wages.

v) Royal Association for Disability And Rehabilitation (RADAR), The Royal National Institute for the Blind (RNIB), Opportunities for People with Disabilities, and similar organisations will provide information on the employment and training of persons with a disability and the financial help that is available.

Grants and practical aid

Grants are available to encourage the employment of disabled people. Disabled persons may apply for help with travel expenses and for equipment which will help them in their ability to work. Financial aid and advice on equipment are also available for the employer:

i) Under the Job Introduction Scheme, run by the Employment Service, a weekly grant is made to employers who take on selected persons for a trial period (usually six weeks). This scheme aims to encourage employers to give persons with a disability a chance to prove their suitability for employment.

ii) For adaptations to premises or equipment a grant is available through the Access to Work Scheme, run by the Employment Service. Adaptations may include the fitting of ramps, special toilet facilities, etc. Persons with a disability can borrow equipment such as typewriters, special seating and desks, or fittings for tools, from the local authority – avoiding the need for an employer to purchase these.

iii) The Disabled Living Foundation, RNIB and other specialist bodies can advise upon aids and office equipment.

iv) Contact your local Training and Enterprise Council (Local Enterprise Company in Scotland) for details of the support they provide for new and expanding businesses.

USEFUL TIPS

- *For both employers and persons with a disability the main point of contact will be the Disability Employment Adviser at your local Job Centre. They can provide advice and contacts on the provision of employment for persons with a disability.*

- *Seek further clarification on the precise requirements of the DDA through expert advice.*

- *When recruiting, specify jobs carefully so that applicants are fairly assessed upon the requirements for that job alone.*

- *Speak to the disabled person about the effects of their disability and what might help.*

- *Make a thorough, realistic assessment of work premises and the attitudes of present employees. The personnel policy should be reviewed and equal opportunities promoted. For any policy to succeed it is important to make it public in a written statement and place responsibility for implementing the policy with a senior manager.*

10 Disability Discrimination Act 1995

This section outlines the main provisions of the Act as they affect employers, businesses providing goods and services, and those letting or selling land and premises.

Introduction

Implementation of The Disability Discrimination Act 1995 (DDA) began on 2 December 1996. The Act introduces new laws and measures aimed at ending discrimination against disabled people. Some changes will come in over a number of years (see Timetable of Implementation below). Except for the provisions on employment, the Act applies to organisations of all sizes.

The Act covers people with learning disabilities, mental illness, hearing and visual impairments as well as people with physical disabilities. It gives them new rights in the areas of employment, in receiving goods and services, and in buying or renting land and property.

According to the DDA, a disabled person is anyone with 'a physical or mental impairment which has a substantial and long-term adverse effect upon his ability to carry out normal day-to-day activities'. A guide to the definition is available. The Act also covers people who have had a disability, but no longer have one.

General measures

i) Under the DDA, it is unlawful to discriminate against a disabled person unless it can be justified. The Act says that it is illegal to discriminate 'for a reason which relates to the disabled person's disability, if he treats him less favourably than he treats or would treat others to whom that reason does not or would not apply'. Discrimination can be 'justified' if the reason for the adverse treatment is both 'material to the circumstances' (ie relevant) and 'substantial'.

ii) A person who allows their representatives (eg sales staff, employees, agents) to discriminate against disabled people would be acting unlawfully under the DDA. If a person can show that they have taken reasonable steps to prevent their representatives from acting unlawfully, then that person won't be considered to have broken the law. The offending representative may remain personally liable.

iii) The DDA makes it unlawful to victimise disabled people who use, or try to use, their rights under the Act. The same protection applies to people who help disabled people complain about discrimination.

iv) The Act doesn't overrule other legislation. If action has to be taken under another law, that law takes priority.

v) The National Disability Council and The Northern Ireland Disability Council were set up to advise the Government on discrimination against disabled people.

Implications for employers

This part of the DDA affects employers with 20 or more staff (including full and part-time permanent staff, temporary workers and workers on contracts). Firms which employ less than 20 employees are exempt from this section of the Act but must comply with all other aspects of the Act. Organisations providing supported employment, along with certain charities, may discriminate in favour of disabled people. The new law doesn't apply to certain groups (eg firefighters, prison officers, police, Armed Forces, and employees working on ships, hovercraft or aircraft).

i) From 2 December 1996 people are no longer registered as disabled and the quota scheme ceased to have effect. Employers covered by the quota scheme at that date must retain quota records until 3 December 1998. People registered as disabled at 12 January 1995 and 2 December 1996 remain registered until December 1999.

ii) Employers are no longer required to reserve job vacancies for car park and passenger lift attendants for disabled people.

iii) Under the DDA, employers must not discriminate against any disabled person without good reason. This applies to all employment matters including recruiting and retaining staff, terms of employment offered, working conditions, promotion or transfer, training, and disciplinary processes.

iv) Employers have a duty to make 'all reasonable adjustments' to buildings, physical features, working arrangements and practices. Adjustments are necessary if the particular disabled person would otherwise be 'at a substantial disadvantage'. Employers are not expected to make changes which would break health and safety laws. If an employer occupies a building under a lease or some other agreement, they should try to obtain approval for physical changes to the property from the relevant person, eg the landlord. A landlord who unreasonably refuses consent may be considered before the Industrial Tribunal and may be liable to compensate the Applicant.

v) Failure to comply with the new duties could result in a case being brought before an Industrial Tribunal. There is no financial maximum on the compensation which can be awarded.

Implications for organisations supplying goods and services

Anyone providing goods, facilities or services to the public will be affected by the Act. This includes commercial businesses and public services, whether they charge fees or not. Discrimination occurs when they refuse to serve a disabled person, offer a disabled person a lower standard of service or less favourable terms, or fail to make alterations to the service or facility, making it impossible, or unreasonably difficult, for a disabled person to use it. If an organisation doesn't own the property from which it operates, then it should approach the relevant person before making physical changes. The DDA doesn't overrule other legislation (eg planning or historic buildings legislation). A limit on the cost of fulfilling the duty to make alterations may be set by the Government. If a feature can't be changed, where reasonable, another way to provide the service to the disabled person should be found.

Disabled access to goods and services

Some changes will come in over time. These will require organisations to take 'reasonable' action to ensure that disabled people have access to their services, goods or facilities by:

a) Making changes to policies, practices or procedures that otherwise make it unreasonably difficult for disabled people to use the service.

b) Trying to obtain aids that will help disabled people use their service.

c) Working to remove or alter a feature of their premises that makes it unreasonably difficult, or impossible, for a disabled person to use the service.

Provision of alternative goods and services

Organisations can provide a different service to disabled people if:

a) Providing the same service would endanger them or other people.

b) The disabled person couldn't enter into a legally enforceable agreement, or give informed consent, and it is a necessary part of the service.

- c) Offering a service to a disabled person would completely ruin the service for others.
- d) Providing a service to disabled people on the same terms as other people meant that the service couldn't be offered at all.
- e) In order to provide a service to a disabled person, a higher charge must be made to cover additional costs.

The Act does not cover private clubs and associations. There are separate rules for education and transport providers.

A Code of Practice is available for firms providing goods, facilities and services.

If a disabled person feels that they have been discriminated against then they can take firms through a county court (England, Wales, Northern Ireland) or a sheriff court (Scotland) in order to seek damages.

Letting or selling land or premises

The Act covers most premises, including land, houses, flats, hostels and business premises.

- i) When letting or selling land or premises, unlawful discrimination could occur if you:
    - a) Offer less favourable terms to a disabled person.

- b) Refuse to sell or let to a disabled person
- c) Treat a disabled person differently on lists
- d) Offer different facilities to a disabled person
- e) Refuse a disabled person access to premises
- f) Evict a disabled person because of their disability
- g) Refuse to give people consent to sub-let to a disabled person.

   It is not, however, necessary to alter the premises in order to make them more accessible to disabled people.

ii) It may be justifiable to treat disabled people differently:
   - a) On health and safety grounds, to protect property and/or other occupants.
   - b) If giving them access to a facility stops others from using it.
   - c) If they must have different access to the facility for others to gain access.
   - d) If they are incapable of entering into a legally enforceable agreement, or giving informed consent.

iii) The Act does not affect landlords, or their immediate family, who let out rooms in their own homes to six or fewer people. Rooms booked in a hotel or a guest house are covered by the part of the Act relating to service providers, but not by the part concerning letting premises.

iv) If a disabled person feels that they have been wrongly excluded from the letting or selling of land or property, they can go to court to seek compensation.

Timetable of implementation

i) From 2 December 1996:

    a) It is unlawful to discriminate against a disabled person in the field of employment.

    b) Employers have a duty to provide any necessary reasonable adjustments for disabled employees and applicants.

    c) It is unlawful to refuse to serve a disabled person, provide a lower standard of service, or offer less favourable terms, because of the disability.

    d) It is unlawful to discriminate against a disabled person when selling or letting land or property.

ii) Provisions affecting service providers for subsequent introduction (timetable may be changed):

   a) (Proposed for 1998) – amend any policies, procedures and practices which make it impossible or unreasonably difficult for disabled people to use the services

   b) (Proposed for 2000) – provide extra help, aids and services to help disabled people get access to the services

   c) (Proposed for 2005) – remove or alter any physical barriers that prevent disabled people gaining access, or provide the service in an alternative way.

USEFUL TIPS

- *Obtain copies of relevant Codes of Practice and Guidance on the definition of disability (see Further Information).*

- *Consider how you may need to change the way you treat customers, employees, and job applicants in the light of the DDA.*

- *Talk to disabled persons about their requirements.*

- *Seek expert advice for clarification on the precise requirements of the Act.*
- *Tell your staff/representatives about the law.*
- *Provide disability awareness training, especially for staff who deal with the public.*

Employer obligations

part
three

11 Contracts and conditions of employment

Introduction

A contract of employment exists when the employee provides acceptance of an employer's terms and conditions of employment by starting work. Both the employer and employee are bound by the terms offered and agreed. The Trade Union Reforms and Employment Rights Act 1993 (TURER) came into effect in October 1994. The Act aims to create a fair balance between protecting the rights of individual employees and avoiding excessive costs and burdens to businesses. Employees now have the right to explicit written details of hours, pay, etc, minimum maternity leave of 14 weeks and better protection against dismissal. There is also better protection against dismissal for exercising statutory employment rights or victimisation for action taken for health and safety reasons.

Contract of employment

A contract is formed as soon as a job has been offered and accepted. In the contract, the company can include specific terms of employment in addition to legal obligations. Terms can be 'expressed' in words or 'implied' by conduct or customs. The contract does not have to be in writing. It may be stated in an interview, or in a letter offering or confirming the job. There are a number of basic requirements for a contract to exist.

i) Offer of employment. There must be an offer of a job by the employer. The offer may be expressed directly or it may be implied. An offer shows willingness to accept the worker. It must be conveyed to the employee. The offer can be withdrawn at any time before acceptance. The withdrawal becomes effective as soon as the employee is notified. There may be time limits to the offer, ie an acceptance must be given within a specified or reasonable period of time.

ii) Acceptance of the offer. There must be an acceptance of the offer by the employee. It can be expressed in writing or orally, or it can be implied. Acceptance must be on the same terms as the offer and be unconditional, ie no changes or counter offers. Modifications can be made to the offer at this stage, but this may result in the previous contract becoming void, and re-negotiations must take place. To be valid, acceptance must be conveyed to the employer.

iii) Consideration. There must be a 'consideration'. This is an obligation binding employer and employee to each other, ie employer's promise to pay and employee's promise to work.

iv) Intention. In order to create legal relations the parties must intend to make a binding employment agreement.

Sources of terms and conditions

The terms and conditions of employment can be found in a number of sources:

i) A specific written contract of employment.

ii) Statutory statement of terms and conditions.

iii) Rule books or policy statements kept by the employer.

iv) An employee handbook.

v) Collective agreements. Abstracts will be incorporated into the individual contracts of employment.

vi) Pension fund documentation. The Social Security Pension Act 1975 stipulates a contracting out certificate. The employer must state in the contract whether it is in force for employment.

In particular, TURER clarifies the position in making reference to other documentation. Most particulars should be written into the statement, rather than given by reference to another document (although this can also be achieved by attaching photocopies of relevant documents). Pension details, sickness entitlement, disciplinary matters and collective agreement documents may be referred to and made available to the employee.

The written statement of employment

After the contract is formed, every employee must be given a written statement of terms and conditions of employment within two months of starting employment. There is no longer a qualifying period (for receiving written details) for those working between eight and sixteen hours a week. Employers must notify employees of any changes 'at the earliest opportunity' and in any event within one month. Under the Trade Union Reform and Employment Rights Act 1993, the written statement must include a number of factors:

i) Names of the employer and the employee.

ii) The position of the employee and job title.

iii) The date the work started.

iv) State whether any other employment is to count as part of the person's continuous period of employment.

v) Hours of work.

vi) How much and when he/she is paid.

vii) Pension rights.

viii) Entitlement to holiday and sick pay.

ix) Length of notice both the employee, and the employer, are entitled to receive.

x) Travel allowances.

Following TURER you must also include:,

xi) Place of work.

xii) Period of employment.

xiii) Summary of duties.

xiv) Collective agreements affecting the employee.

xv) Any periods to be worked outside the UK and any payment changes this may incur.

The Advisory, Conciliation and Arbitration Service (ACAS) Code of Practice, Disciplinary Practice and Procedure in Employment recommends that employers have stated rules of discipline which all employees should know. Rules must be set out in the statement. The code recommends that you state the person to whom the employee can make complaints about conditions of work. Staff are entitled to minimum periods of notice for dismissal and are protected against unfair dismissal. Other sources of information about disciplinary and grievance procedures should be listed, eg in the employee handbook.

Employer duties

The employer has a number of implied duties to employees:

i) Payment of wages, provided the employee does their work.

ii) No work has to be provided as long as wages are paid, unless not providing work will result in no wages, eg the work is on a piece rate basis.

iii) A safe system of work and a safe working environment.

iv) Maintaining a relationship of mutual trust and confidence from both sides.

v) Time off for trade union duties and for public duties.

vi) Disclosure of computerised records under the Data Protection Act 1984 which allows access to data concerning employees and civil remedies in respect to inaccurate data.

Individual employee rights

There are a number of other statutory rights, not necessarily included in the contract; the following list is not complete:

i) A minimum of one weeks notice of termination of employment for each year of continuous employment to a maximum of 12 weeks.

ii) Statutory sick pay of up to 28 weeks per 'period of entitlement'.

iii) No unfair dismissal after two years service (or five years in the case of part-time workers working between eight and 16 hours per week).

iv) Equal pay for equal work.

v) Right not to be discriminated against on the basis of race or sex. This was developed further by TURER. Employees are now allowed to challenge terms in a collective agreement or the rules of an employer which apply to them and which contravene the principle of equal treatment.

vi) Right to take part in trade union activities.

vii) Following TURER all woman are entitled to 14 weeks maternity leave and are protected against dismissal on maternity related grounds irrespective of their length of service. Further, after six months all women employees are entitled to Statutory Maternity Pay for 18 weeks most of which can be recovered by the employer. After two years service all women employees are entitled to a further 29 weeks unpaid absence from work following their confinement.

viii) Continuity of terms and conditions of employment where the ownership of a business is transferred. This may mean extra expense for a business which takes over a privatised or contracted out service.

ix) Additional individual employment rights have been instituted by TURER.

    a) Itemised pay slips must be provided if you have 20 or more employees who work between eight and 16 hours. If you have less than 20 employees they qualify for this right after five years service.

    b) Employees have a right to complain to an industrial tribunal if they are victimised or dismissed when carrying out health and safety duties, acting as a health and safety representative, or bringing health and safety concerns to the employer's attention. You must not dismiss employees for leaving their workplace when faced with serious danger to their health.

c) All employees are permitted to complain to an industrial tribunal. You cannot dismiss employees for asserting their statutory employment rights.

d) A compensation award may be granted to an employee if you refuse to re-engage or reinstate them.

e) The Act has also changed the definition of redundancy along with the laws on consultation with the unions over redundancies. Details of redundancy pay must be given and consultation should be undertaken with a view to reaching agreements.

Restraint of trade

Express terms may be drafted into a Contract of Employment to restrain the employee on termination from using or disclosing the employer's trade secrets or confidential information, soliciting or canvassing the employer's customers or remaining employees, dealing with the employer's suppliers or from generally competing with the employer's business.

Generally speaking, such terms in a contract are void unless the restraint can be shown both to protect the legitimate business interest of the employer and be a reasonable restraint in all the circumstances. In order to be considered reasonable, the restraint must be drafted to afford the employer no more protection than is required to protect his interests.

Essential factors to be considered when determining whether such an express restraint is reasonable are the nature of the business concerned and the scope of the restriction in terms of geographical area and duration of time.

USEFUL TIPS

- *Make contracts clear and easy to understand.*

- *Notify employees of all contractual amendments before they are implemented and make sure they are understood.*

- *An accountant or solicitor will be able to help you draft a standard and specific contract.*

12 Personnel policy statements

Introduction

There are a considerable number of legal obligations on businesses which employ people. Rather than relying solely on a knowledge of the law, it makes sense to prepare a series of personnel policy statements. For many of the requirements, this not only provides evidence that you are complying with the law but also ensures that all your staff understand their rights and obligations.

Writing down a series of statements will help you to think through the way in which you manage your staff and will, in any event, be a requirement if you choose to pursue the international standard of Quality Assurance: ISO 9000. Providing employees with a unified document is also a convenient way to ensure that they receive the information which you are required to give them, and which they will find useful in understanding their relationship with their employer.

Employment policy statement

Very small businesses may not wish to spend the time and effort to develop a employment policy statement. However, once your business starts to grow, it makes considerable sense to develop one.

Why a policy?

The employment policy statement encompasses the principles by which the business recruits, manages and develops its staff. It is closely related to the 'culture and values' of the business. The policy could be regarded as the self-imposed standards which the company adopts in the way it treats its staff (as opposed to standards imposed by the law). Such standards may not always be met, but they are an important statement of intent for a business which aims to achieve high levels of quality. If more than one person is involved in managing staff, it can be useful to have a common point of reference for 'rights and wrongs' if you are to ensure everyone is treated fairly. A clear statement will also help when making comparisons with good practice in other companies.

Contents

A useful way to lay out this statement is to express it as a series of aims or objectives. These will range from expressions of ideals (eg 'Work Organisation – to establish working methods which provide for economic, efficient and satisfying working lives') to specific statements of good practice (eg 'Appraisal to review staff performance at six month intervals').

Other areas to consider for such policy statements are: recruitment and selection, health and safety, pay and conditions of employment, grievance, equal opportunities, communications, consultation and participation, security of employment, appraisal, training, work variation, etc. Examples of policy statements are available from ACAS.

Reviewing policy

It is quite permissible for you simply to write the policy yourself and to impose it on your staff. However, it is likely to be accepted more easily if you involve the staff you already employ in the preparation of the statements. The policy should include a statement about how members of staff can suggest amendments. In addition, you may wish to undertake a more fundamental review periodically.

Policy statements covering legal obligations

Legal obligations

A wide range of legal obligations may be encompassed by your personnel policy statements. If you do not employ anyone in your business (other than your spouse) you need only comply with the Health and Safety at Work Act 1974 (and subsequent regulations) and the Factories Act 1961. No contract of employment is required for the employment of a spouse. If you employ up to five people, you need to comply with the Race Relations Act 1976, Sex Discrimination Act 1986, the Equal Pay Act 1970 and the Equal Pay (Amendment) Regulations 1983. All staff must be given written particulars of terms of employment within two months of starting to work for you; they must be given itemised pay statements and there must be a defined notice period.

If you employ more than five people but no more than 19, in addition to the above, you must prepare and publish a Health and Safety Policy statement. The Factories Act requirements (and also those of the Office, Shops and Railway Premises Act 1963) become stronger. You may dismiss staff only for fair reasons and you have to re-employ staff following maternity leave (Trade Union Reform and Employment Rights

Act 1993). Once you employ 20 people or more, in addition to everything above, you must observe the terms of legislation regarding employment of disabled persons, in particular the Disability Discrimination Act 1995.

Personnel policy statements can help ensure that you are complying with these various laws and regulations.

Basic conditions of employment

Each employee must be given a written statement of the terms and conditions of his/her employment within two months of starting work. This can be done in stages, but there must be a single 'principal statement' which covers: name of employee and employer; dates of start of employment and start of continuous employment; rates of pay and how often payment takes place; specific terms and conditions on hours of work, holiday pay and entitlement; position of the employee and job description; place of work. There must also be general information including sick pay arrangements, pension rights, maternity pay, notice period, etc.

Generally applicable information may be encompassed in a statement of basic conditions of employment applicable to all staff. This can then be supplied as standard along with the particular details of conditions in order to comply with the law. The statement of the terms and conditions of employment is not a contract itself but is evidence of some of the terms and conditions that may be implied in individual contracts of employment. See section eleven 'Contracts and conditions of employment' for details of the information you must provide.

Disciplinary and grievance procedure

Disciplinary rules should also be supplied to new employees. In particular they should state to whom the employee can make any complaints about conditions of work. A statement setting out your approach to disciplinary procedure (which may include a series of verbal, written and final warnings prior to dismissal) and grievance procedures should be produced. Again this may be supplied direct to the new employee, or they may be informed where it may be found, eg in the staff handbook.

See section eighteen 'Disciplining staff' for guidelines on disciplinary procedures.

Health and Safety Policy

Once you employ five or more staff you are obliged to have a Health and Safety Policy although smaller employers may also wish to prepare such a policy. This will normally include a statement setting out the overall obligations on employer and employee. It will set out the way in which the policy should be implemented and will include rules for first aid, accident book, electrical equipment, hazardous environments, investigation of accidents, training in health and safety, etc. Fire instructions may also be included in the personnel policy documentation.

Equal opportunities policy

You should include a statement setting out your policy regarding your approach to equal opportunities. This may deal with the steps you take to prevent discrimination, eg on grounds of sex, age, ethnic origin, disability, ex-offenders, etc.

Other

You may also wish to include statements about particular personnel related issues and procedures such as confidentiality, smoking, total quality management, use of company facilities such as telephone or photocopying, etc.

Distribution

There is no obligation to give every member of staff copies of the personnel policy statements (except for the Health and Safety Policy) though they must be easily available to staff for consultation and they must know where to find them. It makes sense, therefore, simply to give a copy of all personnel policy statements to all your staff.

These documents may usefully be combined into a more substantial staff handbook which might contain other useful information about the business (eg guidance on claiming expenses, procedures on dealing with enquiries, etc). If you do this, you will probably want to ask members of staff to sign a control sheet to acknowledge receipt so that you can prove that the information has been supplied. The law requires that staff are given a copy of the Health and Safety Policy and sign a receipt stating that they have received, read and understood it.

In order to ensure that staff receive all the information they should, it is important to have a clear induction procedure with named persons responsible for providing information. In particular someone should be responsible for providing staff with updated documentation in the event of any changes in policy.

USEFUL TIPS

- *A great deal of help is available to prepare personnel policy statements. Read all the published materials before you start trying to write your own statements.*

- *Involve any staff that you have in the development of the statements since this will make for better acceptance.*

- *If you feel that external assistance would be helpful in preparing statements, do contact your local enterprise agency at an early stage.*

- *Many Training and Enterprise Councils (Local Enterprise Companies in Scotland) offer Business Skills Seminars and other training on employing people. These can provide useful guidelines in this area.*

13 Induction and introduction of new employees

This section suggests methods to ensure that all new employees receive the information and support they need when they begin their new job.

Introduction

Starting a new job can be a challenging, if not traumatic, experience. All too often people tend to treat newcomers with suspicion and in some cases take satisfaction in watching them struggle. This is particularly true for young recruits. A proper approach to induction ensures that the new employee becomes fully effective in their job as quickly as possible and is therefore a cost effective addition to the workforce. It also helps the new employee to feel part of the business, and develops a positive attitude to their job from the outset. If you are working towards the national standard Investors in People (IiP), then developing an induction procedure is an essential part of the process. There is also certain information which you are legally required to give new employees.

General approach

Initial preparations

Make sure that you are well prepared for the new employee's arrival. Other members of the team should be informed, and the workplace should be prepared, eg desk or locker space cleared, keys or passes made ready for issue, so that the new employee has their own space and feels part of the team from the start.

Invest time early on

Plan to invest a lot of time early on with the new person in order to reap dividends later. If they proceed on the basis of false assumptions or wrong information, they will only have to retrace their steps. This is a waste of everyone's time, and the business's money. With the right start the individual will make fewer mistakes in the long run and will need far less support.

Right amount of information at the right time

Do not overload them with information. Do not use your superior knowledge to impress them with what you know. Go at a pace which allows them to absorb the information gradually. The amount of information they receive is less important than how much they understand. If they are just listening all the time they will switch off. Ask questions to establish how much they know, and to get their minds working; they will remember more if they are encouraged to structure their own ideas by talking about them. Pick up on their existing knowledge and expand on it.

Give them something to do

Give them a key task to work on at an early stage. If they do not get a chance to do some work early on they may feel exposed to criticism and not part of the workforce. Work with them closely on the task and enquire about progress frequently. Do not expect too much at first. Treat the first tasks as a learning exercise. Do not set unrealistic deadlines, but be ready to apply more pressure at the appropriate time.

Be flexible

Alter your approach according to the individual. Some will be confident early on. Some will not. Some will appear confident when in fact they are not. Judge individuals by their actions and be prepared to react appropriately. Within reason, tolerate failure. Don't expect too much too soon. It is important to build confidence. Also tolerate a degree of informality with their colleagues. Remember, they are establishing new relationships. Watch out for people trying to take advantage and be prepared to act to support the position of the new person. Be aware that existing employees might feel threatened and be prepared to face up to such issues. Introducing new people changes the team and inevitably causes some disruption. Be prepared for this and accept that new conflicts may arise.

Establish a procedure

Do not re-invent the wheel. When you are happy with your induction procedure set it down in writing. This allows others to benefit from best practice, and speeds up the preparation process. Best practice for introduction to the job should also be set down on paper, usually as part of the personnel policy document. A checklist of areas to cover can help enforce minimum standards. Nonetheless, each induction should take into account the new employee's role and seniority, and any individual requirements.

Ensure responsibility

It should be one person's responsibility to look after the new recruit. Ideally this should be their line manager. It may seem a waste of time to do this, but it is the key relationship to develop, and an investment of time for the manager. All the same, some aspects of information giving may be delegated, and certain individuals may be particularly good at this kind of activity. It may be useful to delegate a member of the new employee's team to look after them at break or lunch periods for the first few days.

Induction

The induction is separate from the introduction to the job in that it is a general programme of 'information giving' designed to ensure all new employees receive certain information. In some circumstances, induction is taken to include certain on the job training (eg machine operatives). This is not covered below.

Administration

Ensure that any outstanding administrative issues are dealt with quickly. These may include supply of the P45, issue of staff handbooks or standard equipment, issue of quality procedures, recording of names on staff notice board, supply of bank details for salary payment, etc. Other basic administration issues should also be covered, eg how to claim expenses, how to get stationery, etc.

Terms and conditions of employment

Check that you have complied with the law in providing suitable job description, letter of appointment, etc. If not, issue these documents immediately. You are required by law to issue employees with a statement of terms and conditions of employment not later than two months after they start work. You should also recap on such basics as hours, pay, breaks, sickness and holiday procedures, grievance and disciplinary procedure, special regulations, etc to prevent any misunderstandings. If the employee will be using a company car, you should deal with any relevant documentation. If there are contracts or agreements to be signed, again this should be done immediately.

Fire and safety precautions

Safety information is particularly important. You are required by law to provide employees with all health and safety information necessary for them to do their jobs safely. Most important is showing them the fire precautions, exits, etc. It may also be necessary to issue a copy of your Health and Safety Policy which the employee must sign and date. Any more specialist safety training or equipment for industrial activities should also be built in.

Office facilities

Show how telephones, copiers and fax machines work. Computer training is increasingly important for most businesses. Give particular attention to data back up and maintenance. Show where everything is kept, and any other premises you use.

Company history and activities

Provide information about what the company does and how it has developed, the market environment, and major competitors. It may help to arrange separate sessions with colleagues to explain different aspects of the business.

Who's who

Go over the structure of the business and provide a list of names and positions. Give particular emphasis to individuals they will be working regularly with. On the first day take them round the company and introduce them informally to everyone.

Sources of information

Staff handbook

The best way to ensure a new employee is issued with everything they need is to develop a staff handbook. This is normally loose-leaf, and contains all relevant information mentioned above (and in this rest of this section). You can also include material such as quality procedures, forms and company strategy. It is also a good place for them to keep their own job details. Someone should be made responsible for compiling and issuing handbooks. The handbook can also be used by the manager in the induction session.

Policy statements

Prepared policy statements can provide useful information about how the company works (eg strategy, targets, etc) and statutory information (eg H & S Policy).

Quality procedures

If the company has implemented quality systems the written procedures will provide essential information. It will also be necessary to give some training in how the system works.

Other sources

Do not overlook the obvious sources including the job description, company brochures and newsletters, and of course the other staff.

Introduction to the job

Introduction to the job is critical. You should have a general discussion to catch up on any developments, news, etc (especially if there has been a relocation). Look out for any domestic difficulties at this stage. How do they feel now that they have committed themselves to this new job? Recap on the kind of issues covered in the job interview. This should be very positive. The person is now in a position to do all the things they talked about at interview. Look again at their personal goals, the goals of the company and goals for the job. Explain how their job 'fits' within company strategy and discuss your policy on training and appraisal. If you are having second thoughts do not show it. Have faith in your decision to employ this person and act accordingly.

Where possible try to involve the employee in planning their own introduction to the job. Some individuals will be able to organise most of it themselves. Build a schedule together and ensure you can check on progress regularly. Give them plenty of context about the company and area of work, especially if they are new to it. Try to balance practical tasks with general discussion.

USEFUL TIPS

- *The induction procedure should begin as early as the initial job advertisement. Ensure that all information you give to applicants offers an honest and accurate picture both of the company and the job.*

- *A follow up interview several weeks into the job can be useful, giving the employee the opportunity to ask any further questions and enabling you to monitor how well the induction procedure has worked.*

- *Some employees, eg school leavers or those who have had a long break from work, may require more support at the induction stage than others. Ensure that you are alert to their needs.*

14 Salaries and other financial rewards

Introduction

In recent years the idea that there should be a standard rate of pay for a particular job has declined. The employment market is more competitive. Collective bargaining has declined in favour of individual agreements. Jobs themselves have become more complex and difficult to define. More participative management styles have opened up new ways to help employees and employers take more informed decisions about financial rewards for work done. Whilst money is not the only thing which employees look for out of their jobs, it obviously plays a vital role. A number of methods can be used to reward performance with money. In the small business, the process of defining financial rewards can be more informal, combining a number of different approaches.

Setting salary levels

A number of different factors will be taken into account when determining salary levels for particular jobs.

Standard rates

In recent years the idea of standard rates for particular jobs has broken down somewhat. Try to pay competitive salaries, especially where the job on offer is widely recognised and has known pay norms. Current levels of salary for particular jobs may be gauged from job advertisements in local papers. Careers directories often list salary levels with career descriptions. Organisations such as employer or trade associations and trade unions will provide information on standard rates of pay. Employment agencies and the CBI can also help.

Budgets

Clearly you can only pay what the business can afford. In times of economic recession employees may be willing to accept lower salary levels than the average if the survival of the business is at stake. Normally, however, you should cost salary levels realistically. Underpaid employees will move on if they can and you will be faced with the continual disruption of recruiting and training replacements. It is a risky strategy to try to undercut competitors by paying low wages. Review staff costs when you review budgets and strategy (usually on an annual basis). Look at what each section of the business can afford, and at differentials between employees. If staff are involved and/or represented in this process, this can ease any negotiating processes.

Differentials

Position and relative responsibilities within the firm should be considered in addition to the standard job. Whilst there may be a standard rate, the person may have additional management responsibilities. Differentials are an important issue. Salary level is not just about achieving a certain standard of living, it is also seen as a measure of the person's worth to the business. It is important to be fair and equitable when one employee is compared to another.

Benefits and conditions

If the job includes a car, clearly it will attract a lower initial salary than an identical job where no car is provided. If the job entails a lot of unpaid overtime or travel for example, the salary might be expected to be higher in recompense.

Prospects

If the job can offer significant prospects within the business, eg future partnership, promotion, etc, this may induce some employees to accept lower rates of pay when they start out. Such conditions are widely abused by employers, so some prospective employees may be put off by vague promises.

Standard of living

One way to think about wage levels is to consider what standard of living, in your area, a certain wage can provide. This can help you decide if you think a certain level of payment is fair for the skills and responsibility shown in the job.

Qualifications and experience

A salary offered will often be adjusted according to the particular skills and experience which the person has to offer. The best type of experience is often considered to be that gained in the job itself. Many firms reward employees for length of service. This discourages experienced people from leaving, which is costly in terms of recruitment and retraining.

If an employee is the best person for the job that they are doing, but has been in that job a while, there is a potential dilemma – especially if you have fixed pay bands. Should you offer them promotion and new tasks, or should you simply try to keep them by paying them more? The answer to this will largely depend on the priorities of the employee – are they ambitious? Or, are they settled in their current post?

Inflation

Many employers seek to maintain the value of salaries by pegging them to inflation. If the value of wages falls, you will have to justify this to your employees.

Salary negotiations

Individual negotiations

Salaries may be reassessed as part of a regular appraisal process. It is particularly important to develop an idea of the employee's expectations. Be frank about the rewards that the business will be able to deliver. Ensure you look at other issues in addition to pay. In medium-sized businesses managers will often negotiate on behalf of their team before the setting of the annual budget. This makes it even more important to have fair and standardised appraisal systems, otherwise wages could be set by negotiating power rather than performance. Once you agree a rate of pay in writing to a new employee it is legally binding.

Collective bargaining

The traditional method of collective bargaining involving trade unions is more common in large companies where many employees are carrying out similar activities. If you employ groups of people who do similar activities (eg data input, print finishing, etc) negotiating rates with a staff representative could save you a lot of time and ensure everyone is on a similar footing. In such businesses you need to pay a lot of attention to staff issues and morale. Disputes and misunderstandings can be reduced if you can find ways to involve the workforce and give them a wider perspective on the business.

Confidentiality

You will have to decide if salary levels for different staff should be confidential or not. If you are in any doubt, consult the employees concerned, but disclosure has to be consistently applied – all or nothing. Whilst most people like to know what others are paid, given the choice they would wish their own salary level to remain confidential.

Commission

Commission may be paid instead of a standard salary or as a bonus on top of a basic wage. This is usually calculated as a percentage of an agreed value such as sales achieved. The percentage may change in return for reaching specific targets. Properly used, they can motivate people to work harder. However, commissions can have the opposite effect if the targets are unrealistic. Bonus commissions are only paid to staff when they have achieved at least their minimum targets. This approach can be useful for boring repetitive work. Commission payments are usually calculated for normal payment periods (eg monthly) which means that the employee is often paid in arrears. Some employers will make a small advance payment to avoid causing financial hardship.

Performance bonuses

Performance related pay is where individuals receive bonus payments for achieving certain agreed targets at work. Bonuses may be annual, but are often based on shorter periods – and sometimes on the time taken to complete particular activities. This approach can be tricky to manage, with staff often ready to exploit loopholes. For example, an engineering firm might allocate a time for each job when costing a contract and award a bonus to staff for every hour the job comes in under time, but without a penalty for going over – the staff may work extra hard to get one job through, attracting a large bonus but neglecting other jobs in the process, perhaps forcing the firm to pay overtime to get all of the jobs out on time.

Profit sharing

Profit Related Pay schemes offer employees limited tax relief (to be phased out by 1 January 2000) on part of their pay which is linked to the profits of the business. Profit Related Pay allows you to reward employees, providing an incentive for all employees to improve the performance of the business and encouraging awareness and understanding of the financial position of the business amongst employees. Schemes may exclude employees with service of less than three years. This could lead to high staff turnover if new employees feel left out, but may encourage experienced staff to stay.

Share option schemes

Companies can offer shares to employees on favourable terms. This is another way to relate rewards to profits and to give employees an interest in the long-term success of the business. There are also tax incentives for this. Some schemes require shares to be held by trustees for a minimum of five years, or give the option to buy shares out of SAYE scheme savings. Many employees find these schemes difficult to understand and prefer benefits with a more immediate return, though they are becoming increasingly common in large businesses.

Pensions

A business can benefit employees by making contributions to their personal pensions. Contributions can be conditional on the employee matching the amount in their own pension contributions, thus encouraging employees to make sufficient provision for the future. Contribution levels can also be related to length of service.

USEFUL TIPS

- *Cost your product or service realistically. Allow for salary levels which you believe are fair and will encourage loyalty and good performance.*

- *Appraise your staff properly, and keep accurate records to ensure you assess and reward performance fairly.*

- *If you can encourage your employees to feel involved in the wider issues of business development, this should encourage realistic wages settlements.*

- *Draw up a policy document on how you go about assessing salary levels. This will help you think the issues through for your own circumstances, and should also help you to implement the principles in a consistent fashion.*

- *Appraisal methods must be fair and objective if you are to reward performance with improved salaries.*

- *It may be difficult to keep varying pay levels confidential and this could cause resentment.*

15 Absence and sickness

Introduction

The absence of employees from work can be a major problem as the business suffers operationally and financially. Employers often have difficulty tackling the problem, and the legal implications can be tricky. Employers need to develop an understanding of the management and legal issues, develop policies and procedures, and apply them consistently and fairly.

Problems

Working relations

Relations with the employee may become strained if there appears to be suspicion or a lack of sympathy. A good working relationship could be spoiled if support is not given when it is needed most. Overall working discipline can be affected if one worker seems to be persistently absent, particularly if they appear to be bending the rules. This will be aggravated if others have to take over the absent person's duties. Employees may become demoralised and others may start to challenge the authority of management.

Operational difficulties

Temporary replacements may have to be hired to cover for absentees. Workloads may have to be redistributed amongst other employees which may result in work becoming disjointed and suffering in terms of quality. At worst, a temporary closure of the business might be necessary if an employee's position in the organisation cannot easily be covered.

Costs

Dealing with the problem of absence may be costly. Management time is required. Dismissal and recruitment have associated costs. If litigation follows dismissal, again there will be costs.

Reasons for absence

Many reasons may be given by employees for absence from work. (NB: absence for reasons related to pregnancy was dealt with earlier).

Normal sickness

All employees suffer the usual ailments related to the British climate such as colds or flu. Employees may on occasions suffer a more serious illness which requires them to be off work for a period of time. Employees should feel comfortable about taking leave when they need to. If they come to work ill, they will suffer in the long run and so will their colleagues. If the general level of sickness seems to be too high, there may be an environmental reason, eg 'sick building syndrome'. Employees should inform their employer immediately when they are unable to attend work, and a record made of the absence.

Persistent sickness

Greater problems arise when an employee seems to be absent for an above average amount of time. The employer needs to establish if the person is genuinely of below average health, if they are hypochondriacs, or if they are deliberately taking advantage of their employer. An employee who suffers from persistent health problems may still be an important asset to the company. It may be necessary to agree special terms and conditions (eg part-time work) in order to be fair to employees who are unable to work normal working hours.

Family sickness

If a member of the employee's family is ill, or there are other difficulties (eg child care problems), an employee may need to take leave. This could become more of an issue as the number of working mothers continues to be on the increase, and parents share the obligations of child care more. Parents usually find a way around such difficulties. The problem can be more of a worry about what they will do should one of their children fall ill for a period of time.

Compassionate leave

Employees may need to be absent from work when there is a death in the family, eg to attend a funeral, and deal with any disruption to family life. The person may also need time off if they are suffering from grief. On occasions an employer may decide to allow leave when an employee is suffering from stress, be it for family or work related reasons. Dealing with stress is a complex issue.

Dismissal

In the eyes of the law persistent absenteeism is classed as 'misconduct'. Long-term absence leads to concern in the area of 'capability'. It is important for continuous consultation to take place between the employer and the individual concerned, and to keep accurate records of decisions reached and agreements made. The degree to which interaction has taken place will affect the decision of a tribunal should a claim of unfair dismissal be made.

Incapability

If an employee's medical condition renders her/him incapable of carrying out their duties to an acceptable standard, then the employer may have grounds for dismissal. The length of absence of an employee before a dismissal is considered fair varies depending on the employee's expected period of absence, sickness record, length of service and the degree of inconvenience caused by the absence. Failure to take any of these into consideration will more than likely result in a tribunal upholding an unfair dismissal claim. Employers may take the option of redeploying the employee to lighter or part-time duties until full recovery has taken place.

Misconduct

If an employee is absent without permission this is clearly a disciplinary matter. An employee may be demotivated through any number of factors such as job content, hours of work and working conditions. The employee may have strong domestic ties or problems which have an effect on their attendance at work. The attitude of a worker towards their job along with the level of employee involvement in their firm will also be an influence.

Statutory sick pay

Employees who are absent through ill health may be entitled to claim Statutory Sick Pay (SSP). This was brought into force by the Social Security and Housing Benefits Act 1982 and covers all employers and employees. The Act states that an employee must form what is referred to as a Period of Incapacity to Work (PIW) in order to be eligible. This is simply the length of time which a worker is absent from work before they can claim financial support through SSP. The PIW must amount to four or more consecutive days. The period of entitlement (POE) does not extend beyond a period of 28 weeks. Employees excluded from entitlement include those on strike, in legal custody, suffering from illness contracted outside the EU, over a pensionable age, receiving certain other benefits and those having completed a full period of entitlement less than 56 days previously. Employees who have not yet started work, along with those working under a standard minimum wage are also ineligible. SSP is treated as earnings so is liable for taxation and the payment of National Insurance contributions. SSP can be withheld in certain circumstances but a statement of reasons must be given on the request of the employee. Under the Statutory Sick Pay Percentage Threshold Order 1995, employers may recover SSP in excess of 13% of their National Insurance contributions in any month. Absence records must be kept accurately and up to date, and evidence of incapacity must be given. Penalties for non-compliance are severe so it is important to know what is required.

Immediate action

Talk to the person at the earliest opportunity. Determine what the problem is. Listen to the person's point of view and ensure they understand your position too. Agree a common approach to the problem. If it is not possible to gain the employee's co-operation, you must be prepared to take the appropriate action.

Frequent short-term absences

If an employee is persistently absent from work for short periods, hold an interview. The aim is to identify the problem, discuss any grievances the employee concerned has and if possible, to find a solution. Absence records should be reviewed, suitable warnings given and opportunities to make representations given in the interview. An option for older employees may be early retirement. This can be a relatively amicable split for both parties although technically it is still considered a dismissal.

Long-term absence

Interview employees who have been absent from the workplace for a lengthy period. The reasons for the absence should be established. If the employee claims to have been absent through ill health then the company may appoint a doctor to examine and prepare a report on the employee on their consent. The employee should be informed as to the risk to their continued employment and a dismissal date should be set if necessary.

Managing absenteeism

It is important also to take more fundamental measures to deal with absenteeism.

i) Monitor attendance. Monitor absenteeism through examining individual absence records. Records can be categorised into sickness, unauthorised absence, holidays and other authorised absence. Weekly attendance records may be an efficient way of carrying out a monitoring process.

ii) Establish procedures to deal with the problem. You should have a specific approach to dealing with absence problems as they arise. This ensures you deal with it promptly, can build upon experience and that you will be consistent and fair. Induction procedures are important too – do employees clearly understand your policy on absence? Someone should be responsible for maintaining written records of absence.

iii) Develop the skills for dealing with such staff problems. It is important to know how to gain trust and encourage people to disclose their problems. If you find it difficult to deal with such issues, can you recruit someone who can?

iv) Review personnel management practices which may impact upon the problem. You may not be selecting the right people for the job. Management may be too autocratic, or perhaps too relaxed.

In the end you have to trust individuals not to exploit sickness leave. Pinning people down in an area where it is difficult to get objective evidence is time-consuming and tricky. Tracking misconduct and disciplining can turn into an expensive game of cat and mouse. It may not be necessary to tackle the problem head-on. If an employee is taking advantage of the sickness system, it is likely that they are bending the rules in other areas of their work. Look at the issue globally. If the person is really difficult you may be able to find another area of their work where it is easier to find grounds for dismissal.

USEFUL TIPS

- *If an employee is persistently absent, investigate and address the problem immediately. If left, things will only get worse.*

- *If absenteeism is a persistent problem, look for the underlying causes, and take action to rectify the problem.*

- *Draw up a clear policy on absenteeism, taking into account any special problems related to your industry, ensure all employees are aware of it, and apply it in a consistent fashion.*

- *If you are on the point of dismissing an employee for health related reasons, take legal advice first.*

16 Employee relations

This section describes ways to develop good relations with employees and, in particular, how to approach relations with trade unions.

Introduction

No business can operate effectively if there is distrust and hostility between managers and staff. Friendly and open relations should lead to higher levels of motivation and should encourage staff to contribute their ideas and observations about how the operation can be improved. Industrial action can be disastrous for a small business. Good employee relations should ensure that disputes can be resolved quickly so that minimal damage is caused.

Employee, or industrial relations may be defined as the rules, practices and conventions governing the relationships between management and workforce. The term industrial relations conjures up a more traditional picture of unionised heavy industry. The smaller business is better placed to establish good employee relations. Everyone can be on first name terms. Many problems can be resolved on a one to one basis. Small firms can react quickly to employee grievances and changing conditions. It is important for the owner manager of a small business to make best use of such opportunities.

Employee representation

Ideally a small business may be viewed as a group of people working together with the common goal of making the business successful. In reality, however, businesses must impose at least some measure of control and discipline upon employees, and frequently employees feel that they need some way to have their own collective interests represented to balance the power of management. Historically, trade unions grew up to take on this role of representing the interests of the workforce. Trade unions developed most powerfully in the large industries, negotiating improved pay and conditions for large workforces in a heavily politicised environment. In the more informal world of the small business introducing union practices can seem like an unnecessary complication. Communication on terms and conditions has to go through the union. Discretionary pay increases based on merit may be hard to implement. Management decisions can be challenged and negotiations may take up an increasing amount of time. Overall, the prized flexibility of the small business may be diminished. Most employers now recognise that fair pay and conditions and fair management are important for business success and actively pursue ways to promote good relations with staff.

Trade unions

Employees normally join unions because they wish to improve their working conditions, usually because the union structure guarantees that they will have a spokesperson. If you are approached to recognise a union or hear talk of such moves, review your own approach to employee relations. Research suggests that certain subjects of dissatisfaction including wages, promotion prospects and job security, are often linked with pressure to unionise. Dissatisfaction with the job itself is not usually an issue. You do not have to recognise a union, but it may be prudent to do so if your employees wish it. If it is not too late, try to negotiate your own alternative consultation procedures. Refusal to recognise a union, or to respond with a suitable alternative, may cause lasting damage to relations with your employees.

Consider the number of unions you recognise. A single union simplifies negotiations but that union has greater power. You can restrict the number of terms and conditions which the union can negotiate. This leaves you with discretion to arrange non-negotiable items directly with the employees concerned. Consider seeking a no-strike agreement with the union or that external arbitration will be sought before a strike is called. You may agree that all employees will be required to join the recognised union or unions – a closed shop agreement. Any closed shop agreement must comply with current legislation.

If you are managing your employee relations well, your employees are unlikely to want union membership. If the subject does come up try to take a positive approach. Create opportunities for the issue to be openly discussed by all staff. Speak to them individually. Is everyone behind membership? Have they thought through all the pros and cons? If the workforce still wish to proceed, work positively with union representatives. Ensure that representatives are from within the business. Do whatever you can to create the right environment for negotiation by marrying union links with your own measures to maintain good employee relations.

Employee representatives

Whether unions play a role or not, many employers see it as good practice to appoint an employee to represent the interests of staff at the management level. Consider allowing a staff representative to sit in on board meetings and be involved in senior management meetings. The person concerned could be selected by the workforce. The representative may be changed on a regular basis. If representatives (union or otherwise) have a good understanding of the needs of the business this should (hopefully) lead to a more responsible attitude if they are involved in negotiating pay and conditions.

Consultation

Consultation before major changes is fundamental. People tend to be unsettled by change, especially if it is sudden and unexpected. More importantly, they may be aware of factors which would have affected the measures implemented. Consultation can be simple, informal discussions. If a decision has been made, eg if a new appointment has been made, ensure everyone knows well before the person starts. More involved consultations may require formal meetings with relevant representatives and the circulation of consultation papers.

Important areas for consultation include working procedures and practices, changes in responsibilities, pay and conditions, major developments in the business (eg change of ownership, acquisitions, etc) and practical changes, eg building alterations, new seating arrangements, etc.

Communication

A great deal of suspicion and distrust can be avoided by keeping staff informed about events. If people feel that they do not know what is going on, they can assume there is something to hide. Information makes people feel secure and more involved in the business's affairs.

Verbal

In the small firm, there is no substitute for talking regularly on a one-to-one basis with staff. People do not always read written circulars. One-to-one, you can make information relevant and gauge understanding. This may happen naturally in the course of work. You may need to arrange to see others that cross your path less often. Confidentiality is important, but try to avoid keeping unnecessary secrets. Avoid a situation where only a select few are 'in the know'. Also, make sure that you listen. You need to find out what others need to know.

Meetings

Meetings, formal or informal, are a valuable communication tool. Small firms can hold meetings of all staff, larger firms may need to organise sub-groups or even a cascade system of briefing. For major announcements a meeting of all staff is usually best. Meetings for particular purposes, eg quality circles, can be used to collect feedback. If people seem to show little interest at meetings, do not abandon the exercise and accuse everyone of apathy. Is there an underlying problem? What can you do to get them more involved?

Written communication

Noticeboards can be useful if they are well located, kept clutter-free, and notices removed when out-of-date. Memos and circulars are a means of directing information to specific people and are especially useful when you need to know that information has been circulated. Do not use these officiously. A common mistake is to circulate a note to all staff when you really need to speak to one person in particular. Consultation papers and reports are of course a very good vehicle for informing people in more depth and can also be used to gather feedback. Ensure that those you circulate with written information are really interested. Consider producing a simple newsletter as a proactive way to keep everyone informed. Handbooks for employees are useful for updating staff on company policy, procedures and activities; particularly useful as part of a quality control system.

Negotiation

There is not room here to look at negotiation techniques in detail, but it may be useful to summarise here the ACAS guidelines for employee representation in small businesses.

i) Establish simple written negotiating procedures, eg employee representative discusses issue with relevant manager; if agreement is not reached, representative meets managing director; if agreement is not reached, conciliation or arbitration may be sought.

ii) Establish clear bargaining arrangements, eg when and how meetings are arranged; who attends and who conducts negotiations; facilities available to representatives; time allowed for trade union or employee group meetings; and procedures for informing staff of agreements or disputes.

iii) Which issues are negotiable and which non-negotiable, should be clearly understood by all parties from the outset.

iv) If agreement cannot be reached, either or both sides may request the conciliation services of ACAS. If there is still no agreement, ACAS can appoint an independent arbitrator, provided the two sides agree to respect the arbitrator's decision.

Reviewing employee relations

If you feel that your business has grown too big for the informal approach, the way you relate to your employees may need more planning and formalisation. Look at the various areas of your activities which impact upon employee relations. As in other policy areas, it helps if you can commit your approach to writing, especially if you wish to discuss and review the policy more widely in the business. The text may form part of your personnel policy document. In particular ensure that you have a suitable grievance and disciplinary procedure in place.

USEFUL TIPS

- *It is crucial to stay in touch with your staff and talk to them regularly, formally and informally. It is all too easy to cut yourself off in a separate office and to blame everything that goes wrong on troublemakers. If necessary get training in employee relations skills.*

- *Establish orderly procedures for collective bargaining and settling disputes. Develop clear, comprehensive and consistent employment policies on recruitment, promotion, training, redundancy, etc.*

- *Avoid giving selected employees special privileges or opportunities.*

- *Under the Social Chapter, legislation will be introduced in the European Community aimed at enforcing certain minimum standards for informing, consulting and involving employees and their representatives. Whilst the UK has opted out of most such provisions, it is still worth noting the importance which the other member states attach to such active measures to maintain good employee relations.*

Effective management

part
four

17 Staff appraisal

Introduction

Once you have recruited staff and delegated tasks to them, you will want to review and appraise their performance regularly. Your staff will want to develop their jobs as part of their career development, so it makes sense to have some sort of appraisal system – formal or informal, or preferably both. Staff appraisals now form part of the British Standard on Quality Assurance and can be useful in establishing a rapport between staff and managers, leading to higher morale and efficiency.

Purpose

Appraisals are carried out for a number of reasons, although these generally fall into the categories of performance, development, communication and reward. Appraisals give you and your staff the opportunity to:

i) Review overall performance during a given period of time.

ii) Ensure a shared understanding of the job and its requirements.

iii) Establish and review the individual's goals and aspirations.

iv) Evaluate current performance by looking at strengths and weaknesses.

v) Let staff know how you think they are doing and find out how they think they are doing.

vi) Talk to each other and establish a relationship based on trust.

vii) Determine how to improve performance by agreeing on an action-plan or a set of goals with an agreed time plan.

Above all, appraisals are a way of maintaining control over the development of the business. The information gained from discussions can prove useful in building a wider picture of the firm. Also, with clearly defined objectives, staff can see how their roles fit into the wider plan for the business. Without such fundamental understanding tasks will lack real commitment.

Aims and objectives

Appraisal systems are designed to help managers encourage people to become more effective in their work. By monitoring performance, managers can be reassured that staff are doing their jobs correctly and that working systems are effective.

You should not adopt a formal system for its own sake; think about what you want appraisals to do before developing a system of your own. The procedure must always be applied with common sense and flexibility. It should not be allowed to become mechanical or be seen as a substitute for informal day to day communication, coaching and constructive criticism.

Informal appraisal should be a continuous process, incorporated into your daily management strategy. If someone performs well, praise immediately. Similarly, poor performance should be discussed as quickly as possible. The aim of appraisal should be to improve performance, not to punish. Keep in contact with staff and note how they work together. Information to be used for an appraisal can be gleaned from colleagues, but this must be seen in the light of the person's relationship with that colleague. Appraisals should provide no surprises, for appraiser or appraisee.

Formal appraisal

Ideally, setting goals and carrying out assessments will become second nature. Staff performance is actually appraised all the time through day to day communication. However, it will still be necessary regularly to assess performance on a more formal basis. Many proprietors do not see a need for this 'because they know what all their staff are like,' but in reality, they are unlikely to carry out a fair and balanced assessment of everyone all the time.

Aim therefore to carry out appraisals regularly. Generally, these are done twice a year, but you must adapt the procedure to your own working patterns; for example a small firm with a rapidly changing workload may need to have appraisals more regularly.

The appraisal form
Some companies prefer managers to write appraisal reports and then discuss them with subordinates. Some ask staff to assess themselves. Many managers prefer to start with a blank sheet of paper. Even if a form is used, be flexible in listening to what the person wants to say. Letting them set their own agenda for the meeting will provide much more information than sticking rigidly to a pre-set format. A standard form will, however, help you to cover all of the points that you wish to discuss.

Preparation for the appraisal discussion
Staff should be given at least two to three days notice of an appraisal discussion so that they have time to consider any points they wish to raise. Ask them to think about previously agreed performance objectives, strengths and weaknesses. If this will be their first official

appraisal, let them see a copy of the form that will be used. If staff are allowed some time to prepare for the interview the discussion should be more fruitful.

Key elements of the job

Decide the criteria on which the individual is being appraised and try to go through them one at a time. Criteria will consist of the most important aspects of the job and should include previously set goals and targets.

Some points which may be useful when considering the appraisee's performance in relation to the key elements of the job are:

a) Job knowledge/application of knowledge.

b) Planning/organisation/administration.

c) Negotiation/cost control/quality control.

d) Innovation/creativity/problem solving.

e) Leadership skills.

f) Working as a member of a team/relations with others.

g) Effective communication/presentation.

h) Acceptance and use of responsibility/coping with pressures.

i) Relationships with those outside the departmental team.

The appraisal interview

This should be a two way discussion allowing both sides to state their feelings and opinions. Record the results of the appraisal, targets that have been set and any performance measures. It is a good idea to begin the interview by looking at the positive aspects of the performance; this will encourage the appraisee to open up about any problem areas further into the discussion. Concentrate upon that person; research has shown that self-assessment by staff is generally accurate when discussions do not ask for a comparison with other colleagues. Try to close with a positive note, giving practical advice and objectives to be reviewed at the next discussion.

Reviewing performance

Summarise the most significant features of the appraisee's performance based on objectives agreed at the last appraisal. Be balanced in appraising the individual's ability; this should form a constructive basis for discussion and encourage them to participate fully in the appraisal interview.

When reviewing past performance it is important to keep in mind that peaks and troughs in performance tend to be most noticeable. If appraisal is continuous and carefully thought out, you should obtain a more accurate picture of the performance.

Performance objectives

Future plans which utilise and develop the skills and abilities of the individual concerned should be agreed. These objectives will form the basis of the next appraisal. Think carefully about the objectives; setting aims beyond the capabilities of the person can result in bad feeling on both sides.

Training recommendations should be made but only where a specific need has been identified and where follow-up action will be taken.

Personal and development needs

The review of performance will have summarised strengths and weaknesses and the agreed performance objectives will have pointed to skills and training requirements. A further part of the appraisal discussion should consider the following points:

a) What can the appraiser do to assist the individual in improving performance?

b) What can the individual do to improve his/her own performance?

c) What formal input (eg training) will help improve the individual's performance?

Generally, most individual's development needs can be met on the job. This might involve some of the following:

a) Coaching by the appraiser.

b) Acquiring new information/skills/techniques.

c) Involvement in problem solving/project work/working parties.

d) Devising and implementing new methods/systems.

e) Undertaking additional/new responsibilities.

Summary of discussion

At the end of the discussion, a summary of the interview should be recorded. This record should contain the individual's reaction to the appraisal, any other important points raised and any further comments or qualifications the individual wishes to be recorded. It is also helpful to write down targets which are set and further needs, such as training, of the person concerned. Provide the member of staff with a copy of the completed form.

Reward systems

Staff will be concerned with their future prospects. The systems of pay and rewards need to be regularly monitored and reviewed to ensure that staff remain in the job. Many systems are available for paying staff, each of which has advantages and disadvantages. The systems include:

i) Time rates, hourly, weekly, monthly.

ii) Individual/group payment by results.

iii) Profit sharing.

iv) Job evaluated structures.

v) Merit rating.

In addition to payment systems, other methods of rewarding staff include holidays, sick pay schemes, pensions and share schemes.

USEFUL TIPS

- *The appraisal process needs to be worthwhile for both participants and must have identifiable outcomes.*

- *Formal performance techniques are unlikely to be appropriate in a small organisation. It is important to develop your own system. One which is unsuitable for your staff needs may lead to misunderstandings and bad feeling.*

- *When making decisions about appropriate systems of reward, it can be helpful to consult the staff concerned.*

- *Never appraise at second hand. Always use personal and authentic experience of an individual's work.*

- *Do not dwell on what has gone wrong, concentrate on why it has gone wrong. Criticism should be constructive, but do not avoid facing a problem if there is one.*

- *Remember that no one works in a vacuum, consider the work and performance in the context of the whole team/department.*

- *Much literature is available giving examples of leading and open questions which can encourage a member of staff to talk openly and honestly about the situation.*

18 Disciplining staff

Introduction

To get the most from your workforce, you need to handle staff problems with care. A failure to do this can result in a lack of staff motivation, respect and loyalty. Problems will, however, inevitably arise, so it is wise to establish the relevant procedures in advance. To handle problems effectively some sort of disciplinary code and grievance procedure is essential.

Disciplinary procedure

To be effective, any disciplinary procedure should be seen to be fair, reasonable, consistent and easy to understand. Employees should be aware of the reasons for a procedure, and it should be both accessible and acceptable to the majority of the workforce.

The first element of any disciplinary procedure involves determining the rules. When drawing up rules and procedures, reference should be made to the ACAS (Advisory, Conciliation and Arbitration Service) Code of Practice on this subject. This sets out guidelines for a fair and 'reasonable' policy on discipline, and is taken as standard in unfair dismissal tribunals. Whilst it is not a statutory requirement that you follow the ACAS Code, adherence will serve to protect your interests in the event of any dispute.

Establishing rules

Although different rules will apply to different types of businesses, their general aims can be summed up as follows:

i) Protection and safety of the person (employee, manager, customer or third party), the business and its resources, products or shareholders.

ii) Creation or regulation of behaviour which ensures that individuals can operate to a degree of mutual satisfaction.

iii) Outlining minimum standards which will ensure the well being of the business.

iv) Prevention of inefficiency or loss.

v) Presentation of the business.

The rules may include duties required by the company health and safety policy, as well as any confidentiality requirements. They may reinforce aspects of the initial contract of employment such as timekeeping or presentation and set standards of customer service which should be maintained. Some reference might be made to major offences such as misuse of company property, violence in the workplace, etc and their seriousness underlined. All rules should be clearly and concisely expressed and should be listed in the company personnel policy or staff handbook, which should be available to all employees.

Drawing up disciplinary procedures

The ACAS Code lists several essential features of a disciplinary procedure. These include:

i) Specifying the levels of management which have authority to take various forms of disciplinary action.

ii) Provision for individuals to be informed of the case against them and to be given the opportunity to state their case before decisions are reached.

iii) The right to be accompanied by a trade union representative or a fellow employee of their choice.

iv) The right to appeal.

Disciplinary procedures should specify to whom they apply and provide for matters to be dealt with quickly.

In addition, a disciplinary procedure should contain:

i) The number of warnings an employee can expect before being dismissed.

ii) The procedure for disciplinary hearings.

iii) How long warnings should remain on record. This may depend on the seriousness of the offence or degree of improvement, but in fairness employees should be able to have their records cleared after a certain period.

iv) A list of offences which may result in summary dismissal (dismissal without warning).

ACAS will normally provide advice on drawing up disciplinary procedures free of charge. Once a procedure has been drawn up, it should always be adhered to. Failure to follow agreed procedures may result in dismissal being held unfair at an industrial tribunal, even if the reason for the dismissal is fair.

Employees should be made familiar with the procedure and with expected standards of conduct and performance. For new employees this should be part of the induction process. Some disciplinary requirements should be included in an employee's contract of employment to satisfy employment and health and safety legislation.

Disciplinary action

When rules have been broken, it will be necessary to follow the disciplinary procedure. When taking disciplinary action the reasons for action should be considered.

It is vital to establish the true facts before taking any disciplinary action, particularly where your attention has been drawn to the situation by someone else, eg a supervisor or manager. Before determining whether formal disciplinary action is appropriate you should talk to the employee face to face, detailing the complaint which has been made and giving them the opportunity to offer an explanation. There may be a problem or obstacle which is causing, or contributing to, the situation, eg personal difficulties or lack of necessary training. The employee may not even have been aware that higher standards of conduct or performance were expected. At this stage, it is important to be sensitive rather than aggressive in tone and to focus on the potential for improvement. Disciplinary action is designed to ensure a return to performance standards which the rules are designed to enforce. You may decide that an informal warning is all that is required, or that further action needs to be taken.

A standard disciplinary procedure will usually incorporate the following sequence of events:

i) A formal oral warning.

ii) A formal written warning.

iii) A final written warning.

iv) Dismissal or other disciplinary action (see below).

Where offences are more serious you may wish to omit stages (i) or (ii). Certain offences are serious enough to warrant summary dismissal (see below).

Disciplinary interviews

All disciplinary action, including warnings, should be preceded by a face to face interview. The following is a basic checklist for disciplinary interviews:

i) Be prepared – gather all of the necessary information before the interview, eg work records, job description.

ii) Familiarise yourself with the possible sanctions available.

iii) Determine who will be present at the interview, eg a colleague of the employee.

The actual interview should involve:

a) Discussion of the situation and clarification of the facts.

b) An agreement on how the situation can be remedied, eg areas of improvement, support required.

c) A plan to monitor future conduct/performance.

d) Setting a time for a further review. This should be realistic in view of the improvement required.

A record of the interview and its conclusions should be kept, and the warning formalised, either orally or in writing. A further interview will assess whether sufficient improvement has been made. Where the employee has significantly remedied his or her conduct it is important to express recognition of their co-operation. Where this is not the case, a further warning should be issued, or more stringent action taken.

Written warnings

Any formal warning (written or oral) should be discussed, and recorded in the employee's personnel file. There should be a period after which the warning is withdrawn from the record. A written warning should specify the nature of the offence or situation and the action which has been agreed to remedy it. It should indicate that a lack of improvement will have more serious consequences. A final written warning should clearly state that further misconduct will result in dismissal.

Dismissal

Dismissal should be the last resort, after a number of warnings, as per procedure, or for an offence leading to summary dismissal. Examples of such offences include violence towards persons or property, gross insubordination, theft, endangering the lives or health of other employees, etc.

Under the Employment Protection (Consolidation) Act 1978 there are five fair reasons for dismissal. These are:

i) A reason related to the capability or qualifications of the employee to do the job for which he or she was hired (this may include the employee's health).

ii) A reason related to the conduct of the employee.

iii) Redundancy.

iv) That the employee could not remain in the position in which s/he was employed without contravening a statute.

v) Any other substantial reason of a kind to justify dismissal.

An employee with two years service or more has a right to ask for a written statement of reasons for dismissal, which must be provided within 14 days of the request. Detailed records of all points at issue and warnings given should be kept. Claims for unfair dismissal can be made by employees with two years continuous service, working at least 16 hours per week (eight hours for employees with five years continuous service).

Other types of disciplinary action

Suspension

Suspension without pay is illegal unless it is a term of the contract of employment. Where it is enforced, the period of suspension is usually between one and four days. Suspension with pay is often used whilst a problem or allegation is being investigated.

Fines and deductions

This, like suspension without pay, can be illegal under certain circumstances. Not being paid for lateness or non-attendance, or for failure to meet stock production levels are examples. Refusal to pay production bonuses, should however, like written warnings, be retrievable in case of performance improvement. In order to impose fines, it must be a term of the contract of employment. If deductions are to be made (eg in the event of stock or revenue deficiencies) refer to the Wages Act 1986 which imposes limitations on this.

Demotion

Demoting a staff member is effectively a breach of contract. The employee has the right to resign and claim constructive dismissal.

Transfer

Unless the employee's contract includes a 'job mobility' clause, transferring them to another location as a disciplinary measure also constitutes breach of contract.

Appeal

Employees should be made aware of their right to appeal against any disciplinary procedures taken against them. Appeals should be made to their immediate manager.

USEFUL TIPS

- *People work best if they are clear about what is expected of them. Ensure your staff understand the duties they need to perform, and your expected standard of behaviour.*

- *Use common sense. Remember that it is your duty to be 'reasonable' – do not make excessive rules and do not try to cover every aspect of work.*

- *Justice must be seen to be done to prevent ill feeling among staff.*

- *Procedures should always emphasise individual improvement and recognise positive efforts. Avoid making them overly negative or intimidating.*

19 Dismissal

Introduction

Dismissing an employee is one of the most difficult things any employer ever has to face. The experience is never comfortable, and it carries a degree of legal risk. Dismissal should not be regarded as a ruthless way to keep employees in check. Difficult and destructive employees can damage the business. Good employees can become unhappy if one person seems to be able to ride roughshod over the rules. The responsible employer must take action in the interests of all concerned. Employment legislation is constantly being reformed and renewed. It is difficult to keep track of the many changes which affect employee rights. It is important to understand when you can dismiss an employee, and how you should do it.

Defining dismissal

Dismissal is said to have occurred when an employer terminates the employment contract, where a fixed term contract expires without renewal, or when the employee terminates the contract in circumstances in which they are allowed to do so. 'Constructive dismissal' occurs when the actions of an employer entitle the employee to terminate the contract. Contracts terminated by mutual consent are not viewed as dismissal, but there must be clear evidence that consent was mutual and that it is not a case of an employee accepting a redundancy offer. Voluntary resignation is not classed as dismissal but if an employee is forced to resign because of an ultimatum given by the employer this is dismissal.

Constructive dismissal

Constructive dismissal occurs where an employee has dismissal rights, even though they may not have been dismissed by their employer. For constructive dismissal to be valid, certain criteria must be met. The employee must prove that the employer was in breach of the contract of service, that it was reasonable that the employee should feel it necessary to resign, that the contract was terminated because of the breach and that the contract was terminated within a reasonable length of time. If the employee delays the decision to terminate employment, they may be found to have reaffirmed it.

Besides breach of written conditions of employment, certain actions of an employer may be seen as breach of the mutual trust and confidence which also form part of the contract.

These include offensive language, sexual harassment, unreasonable accusations of dishonesty and failure to provide reasonable working conditions. If a breach of contract does occur, it is up to the employee to terminate the contract. They must no longer work for the employer, and they must make it clear (by words or conduct) that they do not intend to continue working for them. Notice must be communicated within a reasonable time.

Reasons for dismissal

When an employer dismisses an employee and the dismissal is contested, the employer may have to show that the reason was one allowed by law. These include:

Capability or qualifications

If an employee is not able to fulfil their contract of employment you should be able to dismiss them. Poor performance is not easy to prove. It is important to document when an employee has been asked to do something, and when they have failed to meet reasonable requirements. It is particularly important to use disciplinary procedures. If health is affecting performance, you may need to show that you tried to find an alternative position for the employee before you dismissed them.

Conduct

Bad behaviour (eg offensive or dangerous) needs to be serious and repeated. Summary dismissal occurs when there is a serious misconduct, most commonly fighting in the workplace or theft. Good evidence and information of what constitutes a serious offence should be available (eg in the disciplinary procedure). If an employee is dismissed because of gross misconduct, the dismissal must be communicated within a reasonable length of time.

Redundancy

When making people redundant, you need to show that you have abided by any collective agreements on redundancy selection, and that it is not just a pretext for getting rid of someone. Adequate warning must be given and you should consider alternative employment in the business for the person.

Any other reason for dismissal needs to be substantial, eg you may be forced to dismiss a person because continuing to employ them would breach the law. You should always follow procedures and investigate an alternative to dismissal. If a reason for dismissal exists, the employer would have to show that he acted reasonably in dismissing the employee for that reason.

Unfair dismissal

If you breach your contract (eg unilaterally changing the terms and conditions of employment leading to dismissal) with the employee, they may seek damages for 'wrongful' dismissal in the County or High Courts. Additionally, the Employment Protection (Consolidation) Act 1978 established that employees could also claim 'unfair' dismissal at an industrial tribunal. Unfair dismissal can occur on a number of grounds. It is up to the employer to prove that their action was fair.

Period of employment

In general, persons need to have been in continuous employment for two years or more in order to claim unfair dismissal. This includes part time workers, regardless of number of hours worked per week. There are exceptions (see below). Employees who have passed the retirement age of 65 years may not make a claim for unfair dismissal unless it is associated with a trade union.

Statutory rights

Following the Trade Union Reform and Employment Rights Act (TURER) 1993, it is automatically classed as unfair if you dismiss (or select for redundancy when others in similar circumstances are not selected) an employee for having tried (in good faith) to assert one of their statutory employment protection rights (eg by bringing proceedings against you) even if they did not actually qualify for that right or the right in question was not actually infringed.

Pregnancy

Following TURER all women are protected against dismissal on maternity related grounds in that dismissals due to pregnancy are automatically unfair irrespective of length of service or hours of work. A woman should be offered alternative work (where there is a suitable vacancy) or suspended on full pay if she cannot return.

Health and safety

All employees, regardless of length of service or hours of work, have the right to complain to an industrial tribunal if they are dismissed for carrying out designated health and safety duties or acting as an official health and safety representative. They can also complain if dismissed for bringing a reasonable health and safety concern to the employer's attention (in the absence of a representative), or for leaving the work area or taking action to protect themselves and others when faced with serious or imminent danger.

Trade unions

Dismissal for trade union membership, activities or for refusal to join a trade union may be unfair. No qualifying period is required before claims can be made. The employee must prove the relationship between the dismissal and trade union membership.

For valid claims an industrial tribunal can order reinstatement into the position the employee was dismissed from, re-engagement into a comparable position or monetary compensation for the loss of employment. There are limits on the amount of compensation which the tribunal can award, which may be exceeded in certain cases where reinstatement or re-engagement orders have not been fully complied with.

Communicating dismissal

The general rule is that once a dismissal has been communicated, it cannot be withdrawn without the consent of the other party. If there is any ambiguity in the words used certain rules must be applied to assess the validity of the comments. If the words are said in the heat of the moment, then they may not always be taken at face value and withdrawal should be communicated within a reasonable length of time. Employers must also give due consideration to mentally unstable employees. If dismissal is communicated in writing, you must ensure that the letter is unambiguous and clearly indicates the date of termination.

If an employee requests a written statement of reasons for dismissal, the employer is required by law to give that statement within 14 days. Only employees who have been in continuous employment for a minimum of two years have the right to demand this statement. If the statement is not provided, or is inaccurate, the employee could present a complaint to an industrial tribunal (details given should be exactly the same as those given to a tribunal if you are to stand any chance in a hearing).

Statutory minimum notice period

Periods of notice are normally given on the written particulars of employment, but there are statutory minimum periods. If someone has been employed for longer than one month then according to the Employment Protection Consolidation Act (EPCA) 1978, they are entitled to be given the following:

i) One weeks notice for less than two years continuous employment.

ii) An additional weeks notice for every continuous years employment between two and 12 years.

iii) No less than 12 weeks notice if the employee has been in continuous employment for more than 12 years.

Statutory minimum pay during notice

Employees have the right to statutory minimum pay throughout their notice period unless: they are validly dismissed during the notice period; they go on strike after giving notice; or they are granted leave of absence during the notice period. The employee is entitled to payment for the number of hours worked. If the hours are not actually worked they are still entitled to be paid if they are taking due holidays, they cannot work due to injury or if they are prepared to work but no work is given.

Disciplinary procedures

Following disciplinary procedures is very important to ensure that dismissal is fair. In most cases, employees are made aware of any procedures when they receive their conditions of employment. Procedures help you to stay within the law, treat the employee fairly and compile any evidence that you might need to use in the event of a dispute. Procedures should ensure that employees are aware of the complaint being brought against them. They should have the opportunity to put their case forward and the employer should act in good faith.

The first breach of contract is not normally serious enough to warrant a direct dismissal. There is normally an oral warning, followed by a formal written warning before any dismissal. It is important that formal records are kept of all warnings and correspondence (you may choose to ask the employee to sign for letters). The final written warning should state that the next disciplinary procedure will come in the form of a dismissal action. The duration of a warning will normally depend on the seriousness of the offence. Alternatives to warnings include suspension, transfer, demotion or loss of privileges.

USEFUL TIPS

- *Ensure that you have suitable disciplinary procedures in place. This will help you comply with the law where dismissal arises from disciplinary problems.*

- *Act decisively. If it seems that you will have to dismiss an employee, do not prevaricate. Tackle the problem immediately but always consider obtaining legal advice first.*

20 Redundancy

Introduction

Redundancy is an emotive subject. Loss of employment is a severe blow for individuals and their families. At the same time, failure to take prompt action may lead to complete business failure. You need to be aware of these issues if you are considering making staff redundant. Your decisions should be based on a rational assessment of the long-term needs of the business, and the requirements of current employment legislation.

What is redundancy?

There are a number of circumstances in which a dismissal may be classed as redundancy.

i) The business employing the worker ceases trading, or intends to do so.

ii) The type of work the person was employed to do is scaled down or ceases.

iii) The worker becomes surplus to requirements through a factor affecting the tasks undertaken by that individual (eg, being replaced by a machine).

iv) The business employing the worker ceases (or intends to cease) operations at the site where the worker is employed (refusal to move to nearby premises may not entail redundancy, eg if accessibility is an issue).

The main feature of redundancy is that an employer has had to reduce their workforce in some way. To be redundant, a worker's job must have disappeared, even if the employer is recruiting in other areas. If a worker's job is taken over by another employee, redundancy is still valid if that employee's job is then vacant or there is a net loss of jobs.

Some workers have contracts that allow periods laid off without pay, or on short-time working (earning less than half a weeks pay). They can claim to have been made redundant if they have been laid-off or put on short-time working either continuously for four or more weeks, or for any six weeks out of thirteen. The worker must notify the employer of the claim in writing within four weeks of the end of the period. The employer has seven days from receipt of notice in which they may notify the worker of a 13 consecutive week period of employment expected to start within four weeks. If this new period of employment is not forthcoming, the worker can be classed as redundant.

Entitlement to redundancy payments

Employees (meeting qualifying criteria) are entitled to redundancy payments; the self-employed and members of partnerships are not. Directors may qualify if they have contracts of employment, but not if they work on a fee basis. Employees of normal retirement age are not entitled to redundancy payments, nor are apprentices whose period of service ends at the same time as their apprenticeship contract.

Qualifying periods

Since February 1995 the qualifying period is two years for all employees, irrespective of the number of hours worked per week. Service only counts after 18 years of age. Employment Department booklet PL711 details the rules governing continuous employment.

Continuity of service

Time counted as continuous is subject to various conditions. Work for a previous employer may count (eg if the business transfers ownership, or if the employee changes companies but the firms are under the same ownership). Contracts where the employee normally works outside Great Britain do not give that employee entitlement to redundancy payments; but if the employment conditions change and the employee works within Great Britain for the same employer, the previous overseas service will count towards the period of continuous service. The number of hours contracted for, and worked, in a week have a bearing on qualifying periods. Strikes do not affect continuity of service, but the number of days on strike can be deducted from the total number of days served when calculating length of service.

Fixed term contracts

A fixed term contract of two years or more which ends without renewal may entitle the employee to a redundancy payment unless the contract included a waiver clause and the employee gave written agreement to it.

Alternative offers of employment

Offers of alternative employment with the same or an associated employer, or with a new employer taking over the business, may remove entitlement to redundancy payments. This happens if the offer is made before the old contract ends, provided the new contract starts within four weeks. The employee may choose to try the alternative post for up to four weeks before accepting or rejecting the offer. If the alternative is unsuitable, or there are valid reasons why an employee cannot take up the offer, the employee is deemed to have been redundant from the original date that employment ended. Employees unreasonably rejecting offers of employment lose their entitlement to redundancy payments. If employees are made redundant when a business is transferred it becomes unclear whether the old or the new employer is liable to make payments. Any dispute over entitlement to a redundancy payment can be referred to an industrial tribunal if it is not settled earlier in consultation or arbitration.

Calculating redundancy payments

A statutory redundancy payment to an employee is not taxable as income, though it is a business expense for the employer and can be set against tax.

Calculation of redundancy payments is based on length of service, number of years served in particular age bands, and on the weekly pay. Statutory entitlement starts at two years continuous service. The maximum payment is for 20 years continuous service. Length of service is reduced by the number of days an employee has been on strike, and lengthened by the number of days notice due but not given.

There are three age bands, with entitlement ranges from half to one and a half weeks pay for each year worked in a band. A weeks pay normally means the payment due for basic contracted hours, though in some instances regular overtime and bonuses may be included. The payment entitlement of employees approaching their 65th birthday reduces by a twelfth for each month after their 64th birthday. Entitlement reaches zero when they reach normal retirement age. When the employer pays the redundancy payment, the employee must be given a written statement setting out the calculation for payment.

Calculating entitlement and payments can be complicated. The Employment Service booklets on the subject give the precise and up to date criteria. Disputes can arise over any aspect of continuity of service or the value of a weeks pay. Any such dispute can be referred to an industrial tribunal and/or ACAS.

Handling redundancies

Forward planning

Making employees redundant can be unpleasant. The problems are minimised where redundancy falls at the end of fixed term contracts, provided employees do not expect renewal of contract. Early awareness of a need to reduce staff or introduce new working methods will let you plan the workforce changes required and implement retraining or to allow natural wastage and a freeze on recruitment. Planning ahead makes it possible to consider the needs of the business beyond the immediate crisis and to ensure that the right staff are in place for the recovery. The blow can be softened by giving the employees concerned as much warning as possible and making sure that they hear it first from you. Consider the effects of rumour and adverse publicity on customer and supplier attitudes.

Notification

An employer must notify the Department of Trade and Industry (on a form obtainable from any Job Centre or Unemployment Benefit Office) if he proposes to make 20 or more people redundant within a period of 90 days. Notification should be received by the Department at least 30 days before the redundancies occur. You need not notify the Department of fewer than 10 redundancies, though it may be prudent if the number might rise to ten or more. Redundancies of 100 or more workers within 90 days require at least 90 days notice. Failure to notify will lead the employer to be liable to a fine.

Consultation

Copies of any notification of proposed redundancy must be given to representatives of any trade unions that you recognise – whether or not the employee to be made redundant is a member of a trade union, provided that an employee of the same description is a trade union member. The employer must also inform the union in writing of various aspects of the redundancies including: reasons behind them; method of employee selection; proposed method of carrying out dismissal; number and description of employees; proposed method of calculating non-statutory redundancy payment; total number of employees of any such description employed at the establishment in question. Periods of consultation are the same as for periods of notice to be given to the DTI. Aim for full consultation with the union before individual redundancies are finalised to see if the number of redundancies can be lowered. Consultation can lessen the effects of redundancy directly because management and employees are seen to tackle problems together and effective measures may be agreed. If the employer proposes fewer than 20 dismissals within 90 days, there is no direct duty to consult, but consultation is still advisable to prevent a redundancy dismissal from being rendered unfair.

Notice to staff

Once it is certain that redundancies will occur, due notice must be given to the selected staff, or payment in lieu of notice should be arranged. Statutory minimum notice periods apply unless contracts of employment require longer. After one months service, one weeks notice is due; after two years, two weeks are due – thereafter the period of notice is one week for every year worked, up to a maximum of 12 weeks.

Selecting staff

The selection of personnel for redundancy has to be done carefully so that you avoid claims of discrimination or unfair dismissal. Volunteers should be considered first, bearing in mind that some may have experience or skills that you do not want to lose. When deciding on compulsory redundancies, the process should be fair. Take into account length of service, performance and possibilities for retraining. If it is customary for your firm to use a last in, first out process, it may be unfair to change. Give affected staff time during work hours to look for alternative employment or find training options. Some firms will use contacts and Job Centres to help find new positions and provide job search facilities such as telephone, photocopier and a word processed CV.

Payment problems

If serious cash-flow problems threaten the business, and making redundancy payments would push the firm over the edge, redundancy payments may be arranged by the DTI from the National Insurance Fund. To get such assistance, you must show that no more credit is available to you. You need to repay the amount as soon as possible. If insolvency occurs, the Department claims repayment from the assets of the business.

USEFUL TIPS

- *Do not put off necessary redundancies. The business may be damaged further and more jobs could be lost in the long run.*

- *The regulations dealt with in this section cover statutory minimum periods of notice and payments. A company can improve upon these conditions if it wishes.*

21 Handling conflict between employees

Introduction

The impact of poor relations between staff can be devastating, especially in a small organisation where the few employees all make significant contributions to the success of the business. Small workplaces generally have better relations, but when problems do arise they can have far greater impact because employees may be working closely in contact with a few people. Conflict can have both an invisible and a visible impact, anything from non co-operation to fighting on the factory floor.

The problems can be hard to deal with; not only are there procedures to follow and legislation to adhere to, but the source of the conflict itself may be hard to identify and quantify. Often it is only when the effects of conflict become clearly evident that anything is done. Conflict can escalate easily if both sides start looking for further real or imagined breaches of behavioural standards to reinforce their impression of the other.

There are three aspects to conflict – how the parties behave to each other, how they behave to other people and what the consequences of their behaviour are. These factors will determine the scope of action which can be taken to rectify the situation. A manager should view conflict as an opportunity to improve communication and relations between the protagonists – and throughout the business.

Types of conflict

i) Between manager and staff – this can result in a communication breakdown. Service for customers may be reduced if staff are less helpful as a way of getting back at the manager. Non co-operation can undermine the authority of the manager. A manager may cause problems for staff by threatening to block promotion, etc. This is especially dangerous as power is involved; even if both parties are equally to blame, the situation is weighted in the manager's favour.

ii) Between employees – this can cause major problems if they are badmouthing, conducting arguments in front of customers, or refusing to communicate. Health and safety and the viability of the business can be compromised.

Reasons for conflict

i) Personal – this can be a personal problem such as a basic personality clash, a personal argument or a relationship gone sour; the result of a personality defect in the aggressor such as bullying, bearing grudges or picking fights; or even the result of rumours.

ii) Professional – this can be because of fear of change (eg in personnel or work methods). Alternatively, conflict could be the result of different ideas of working, directions the business should be going, feeling that other workers do not have the interests of the business at heart, etc.

Healthy and unhealthy conflict

i) Consequences of healthy conflict – even on a personal level between two employees, conflict can be healthy. Rivalry and competition can cause people to put forward and debate ideas. It can increase productivity, assertiveness and self-esteem in staff. Such an environment can lower stress levels and help the business in many ways.

ii) Consequences of unhealthy conflict – unhealthy conflict, aggression and bullying make staff less productive (aggressor and victim), drain people of energy, cause an atmosphere of fear and mistrust, stop discussion, and damage self-esteem. Personality clashes use up energy on trivial matters with no benefits. It can cause distress for those involved, lead to stress related illnesses, increased absenteeism, etc. There is also the inconvenience for those indirectly affected (eg when important information is not passed on or acted upon). The business will not function as well and profits may be affected.

Ways of preventing conflict in the long term

There will always be people who are combative, or who don't get on with specific people or other people in general – so there is always the possibility of conflict in the workplace. However these traits and circumstances can be lessened or even used to the advantage of the business.

i) Communication – by regularly having one-to-one talks with staff, you will be able to spot problems building up, and see how staff relationships are going. Communication settles staff problems more easily. Regular staff meetings encourage team spirit. Ensure that employees are aware of the aims of the business and where they fit into them.

ii) Look at the business's management style – is the atmosphere or conflict the result of the management or business style (eg does it appear that some issues are not open to discussion?). If people feel the only way to get ahead is to intimidate others, it may be because that is how they see others act. If employees know that you are a fair manager, will not take sides, and are prepared to listen and offer support, any conflict that does arise is more likely to be sorted out before it causes serious problems.

iii) Encourage team work – a sense of common purpose can prevent conflict or lessen its worst effects. Hostility is often caused because people are scared of the unknown, so if someone seems like a rising star, or appears to be after another employee's job, staff may fear them and their motives and feel they have to 'attack' first.

iv) Set professional standards – behavioural standards should be known and accepted by all employees. Always emphasise that employees must observe the standards of behaviour.

v) Have formal procedures – standard rules and grievance procedures make dealing with the results of conflict much easier, as long as staff know that they will be rigidly followed in the event of continued problems and complaints. Point out the procedure that will be followed if an incident re-occurs, then carry it out if necessary. Most grievances are solved at the first stage of a grievance procedure.

Ways of dealing with conflict when it arises

The options for action depend on the type of conflict. If the conflict is work related, as a manager you may be able to diffuse the situation. If the dispute is personal, avoid getting involved in reasons and arguments. It is not your job to make them best friends, but you must limit the effects of any dispute on the business.

i) Talk to each party separately. An informal, private, frank discussion may be enough. Listen to them. Talk in a neutral, non-attacking way. Make sure that you use an authoritative voice, make lots of eye contact, and don't be seen as weak or a 'soft touch'. Don't acknowledge bad behaviour, as it reinforces it as an attention-seeking device.

    a) Let them air their grievances, but don't respond to them. Ignore attacks directed at either you or each other. Ask questions, see if they want to talk about anything. Problems could be personal or work-related. Look for clues to greater problems – they may first admit to some minor problem, but be hinting at the real, more serious reason for the conflict. Give a serious response, don't trivialise the problem. Make it clear that they can discuss the situation, but if they refuse and do not behave in a more professional manner it becomes a work problem and they will be disciplined. Emphasise professional standards.

b) Help them to deal with the problem, even if the first step is just to explore possible solutions rather than actually solving it, so that something is clearly achieved by the meeting. If it is a personal problem, encourage them to make their own decisions as to what they do.

c) As a manager, try not to get involved on a personal level – your business is to work on the consequences of their behaviour, not the reasons behind it.

ii) Make them communicate. Plan a weekly meeting with both parties until it is clear that communication is okay between them and a satisfactory professional relationship has been established.

iii) Make them work together. In some situations it may pay to insist that people work together on projects. This can harness their antagonism and can lead to debate within the project, and therefore benefit the firm. You should use meetings to keep up with progress, and make sure that the project involves them liaising with each other rather than just each completing their own work. At meetings, question them about each other's work on the project, so you know they are really talking.

iv) Remove the problem. Consider offering a voluntary transfer to one worker, if there is a post for them to go to. This is useful if there is a deep rooted personality clash or aggression by one party.

v) Take disciplinary action. You may have to use discipline, not only to prevent them doing it again, but to show others that unprofessional behaviour is not acceptable. Usually, conflict is reciprocated. If both are clearly to blame, then warn both, and if warnings are not heeded then (with reference to employment legislation) it may be necessary to dismiss them. If one is more to blame than another, you may have to dismiss that person and warn the other. Usually, it takes two people to cause a disagreement, but if one person is picking on another, then a system of warnings and possibly eventual dismissal may be the only way. If fighting or other gross misconduct is involved, summary dismissal may be in order. You should be sure you know who is in the wrong before you act.

USEFUL TIPS

- *Try to limit your involvement in any problem to how it affects the business. You can be sympathetic to the personal problems of staff, but you should keep a distance.*

- *Ensure your business has a policy for grievances and problems, and make sure staff know about it.*

- *Communication is the key; it won't necessarily prevent personality clashes, but it contributes to an atmosphere of openness and makes employee conflict easier to deal with.*

- *If you have to take disciplinary action, make sure it is based on business reasons and not personal ones. If your action is discriminatory or does not comply with established grievance procedures you may face a claim of unfair or constructive dismissal.*

Trade unions and industrial relations

part five

22 Trade unions and the law

Introduction

Trade unions aim to improve pay and working conditions and generally to protect the interests of their members (eg health and safety, pensions, security, etc). Many managers of small businesses have had little direct contact with unions. They and their employees often feel that unions are an irrelevance due to the size of their business. There can, however, be advantages. For instance when discussing pay you may find negotiating with a single representative and entering into formal agreements easier than negotiating individual employee contracts.

The Trade Union Reform and Employment Rights (TURER) Act 1993 included various provisions on trade unions and industrial action. Individuals now have more freedom to choose which trade union they wish to join. More union information will be disclosed and consent must be obtained before union subscriptions are deducted from pay. The Act also provides for industrial action ballots conducted by fully-postal voting. Individuals will be able to exercise 'Citizens Right' which enables them to stop unlawfully organised industrial action with the help of an independent commissioner.

Employer obligations

There is no legal obligation to recognise a union. If you do recognise a union, certain obligations are immediately imposed upon you. For instance, if a shop steward is appointed, he/she is entitled to reasonable time off work for trade union duties and activities. You are expected to keep the union informed of new company projects and you are under a duty to consult them if you dismiss for redundancy a union member. During a period of collective bargaining it is the employer's duty to disclose to representatives of a recognised trade union any information without which they would both impede union officials and damage industrial relations. In any event, it is sensible to promote good industrial relations without recourse to the law.

More information must now be published by the unions including financial information such as pay and benefits of its leaders and annual written statements. The appointment of a certification officer means that the trade union's financial affairs can be investigated.

Membership

Employees can belong to any trade union they like except where membership is limited to particular occupations, skills, geographical area, or if the employee's conduct is unacceptable. If an employee is unlawfully excluded or expelled, they can complain to an industrial tribunal.

Membership dues can only be deducted with the employee's written permission. This must be renewed every three years or when the rate changes, and the employee must be given one months notice of this by the employer, with a reminder of the member's right to withdraw. Trade unions cannot expel a member for leaving this system, joining any other union or for being a non-member. Employees can complain to an industrial tribunal if wrongful deductions are made.

The Trade Union and Labour Relations Act 1992 made it unlawful to threaten industrial action to establish or maintain any sort of union closed shop practice. A closed shop, as such, is not illegal but it cannot be enforced.

Health and safety

Employers are required to appoint safety representatives in each area of work, unionised or otherwise, according to the Health and Safety at Work Act 1974. If a trade union is recognised it can appoint safety representatives. How it appoints the representatives is a matter for the union. The safety representatives must be given time off work to undergo training and to fulfil their functions. These include:

i) Investigation of accidents, dangerous occurrences and hazards. Notification of these situations to the manager.

ii) Meeting relevant outside inspectors.

iii) Formal inspections of the workplace every three months or following accidents.

iv) Inspecting and keeping copies of relevant documentation kept by the employer.

Under TURER, your employees have the right to complain to an industrial tribunal if they are victimised or dismissed when carrying out health and safety duties. You cannot dismiss employees for leaving the workplace when faced with a serious danger to their health.

Industrial action

A person or trade union who calls for, or threatens to call for, industrial action only has legal immunity if acting in contemplation or furtherance of a 'trade dispute'. The official definition of what constitutes a trade dispute is long and complex but, briefly, two main conditions must be satisfied. It must be a dispute between workers and their own employer and the dispute must be wholly or mainly about employment related matters. A trade union needs to give an employer seven days notice of industrial action in writing.

If a trade union calls on its members to take industrial action, it will have no legal immunity unless it holds a properly conducted secret ballot and secures a majority of its members in support. Any individual who claims that unlawful industrial action by a trade union will lead to the prevention or delay of the supply of goods and services can take legal action, irrespective of the effect of that action on the individual. An independent commissioner can be appointed who may help the individual exercise this right.

A union can be held responsible for the unofficial action of its members where the appropriate official does not act decisively to communicate the union's official policy to its members, although the union may avoid liability by repudiating the act within a reasonable time period. Trade disputes are now classed as private disputes between you and your workforce. Employees cannot bring in outsiders for consultation during discussions with you.

Peaceful picketing is allowed. Government codes of practice suggest it will be rare for the number of pickets to exceed six. Picketing should be at or near the place of work. It should be connected to the trade dispute and should be only peacefully to inform or persuade others and not to intimidate them. Pickets are allowed to reason peacefully with workers in an attempt to persuade them to join in with the industrial action. Union officials are permitted to visit pickets to give them moral support. Secondary action involving the business' commercial contacts is illegal.

Ballots

Following TURER, in order for a union to retain its immunity from civil action all industrial action ballots must be conducted by fully-postal voting. Seven days notice of the ballot must be given by the trade union and you are entitled to see the full results and sample voting papers. Ballots of more than 50 members will be scrutinised more closely and the results made available to employers and members within a month of the ballot.

Small businesses employing less than 20 staff are exempt from requirements to permit their premises to be used by union members for a secret ballot.

Union merger, election and political funding ballots must all be conducted by fully-postal voting. Trade unions are not allowed to distribute material which may influence voting in merger ballots.

Employment legislation regarding trade unions is complex and is continually changing. The following points should be borne in mind:

USEFUL TIPS

- *If you do become involved in a dispute, try to resolve it locally through procedures agreed with the recognised union. If this fails, consider using ACAS as an arbitrator. The majority of ACAS negotiations are on behalf of small and medium sized companies. Following TURER, charges may now be made for some ACAS services.*

- *Useful information regarding disciplinary procedures and what is considered reasonable disclosure of information to a union when involved in collective bargaining can be obtained from the ACAS codes of practice.*

- *If you know that a union has acted unlawfully, eg by not balloting over industrial action or participating in secondary action, always obtain legal advice before starting legal proceedings.*

23 The Trade Union Reform and Employment Rights Act 1993

This section looks at how the Trade Union Reform and Employment Rights (TURER) Act 1993 affects the small business. It provides general guidance only and is not intended to be a comprehensive statement of the law.

Introduction

The provisions of TURER came fully into effect in October 1994. The Act aims to create a fair balance between protecting the rights of individual employees and avoiding excessive costs and burdens to business. Many of the provisions of the Act are an implementation of the EC Directive on Proof of Employment Relationships 91/533, and bring the UK further into line with other European countries.

Main provisions

Individual employment rights

Employees now have the right to explicit written details of hours, pay, etc, minimum maternity leave of 14 weeks and better protection against dismissal. There is also protection against dismissal for exercising statutory employment rights, or victimisation for action taken for health and safety reasons. Part-time employee rights are improved.

Trade unions and industrial action

Individuals now have more freedom to choose which trade union they wish to join. More union information should be disclosed and consent must be obtained before union subscriptions are deducted from pay. The Act also provides for industrial action ballots conducted by fully-postal voting. Individuals are able to exercise 'Citizens Right', which enables them to stop unlawfully organised industrial action with the help of an independent commissioner.

Other provisions

The Act also abolished wages councils and minimum payment rates. The Careers Service now offers a more flexible and responsive service for the local community. The Act also extends most of these rights to the Armed Forces.

Individual employment rights

Written employment particulars

New employees are entitled to a written statement of the main employment terms within two months of starting work. Existing employees are similarly entitled upon request. Any subsequent changes must also be notified to employees within one month. The statement must include:

a) The names of the employer and employee.

b) The date when the employment began.

c) The date on which the employee's period of continuous employment began.

d) The scale or rate of remuneration or the method of calculation.

e) The intervals at which remuneration is paid.

f) Hours of work.

g) Holiday entitlement.

h) Sickness entitlement.

i) Details of any pension schemes.

j) The notice which the employee is obliged to give and entitled to receive to terminate his/her employment.

k) The job title or a brief job description.

l) Where the employment is not intended to be permanent, the period for which it is expected to continue or, if it is for a fixed term, the date when it is to end.

m) Place of work.

n) Details of any collective agreements affecting the terms of employment.

o) A note containing details of grievance procedures and (except in firms with fewer than 20 employees) disciplinary procedures, and stating whether a pensions contracting-out certificate is in force.

Where an employee, who normally works in the UK, is required to work abroad for a period, the statement must also cover the duration of the period, the currency to be paid, any additional pay or benefits and the terms relating to the return to the UK.

The statement may refer to separate 'reasonably accessible' documents for details of sickness entitlement, pension schemes, grievance/disciplinary procedures or provisions which are covered by the law or collective agreement in relation to notice entitlement.

Itemised pay slips

If you have 20 or more employees, you must provide pay slips to those who work between eight and sixteen hours. If you have less than 20 employees, those who work between 8 and 16 hours qualify after five years service.

Maternity rights

a) All women, regardless of length or service or hours of work, are entitled to 14 weeks statutory maternity leave and to receive all their normal conditions of employment during this period, except pay. The right to maternity absence of up to 29 weeks after childbirth remains.

b) The dismissal of a woman will be automatically unfair if it is on maternity-related grounds.

c) If a woman has to be suspended from work for health and safety reasons, she must be offered suitable alternative work where possible, or if not available, suspension on full pay.

Health and safety rights

Dismissal, selection for redundancy or victimisation will be automatically unfair if the reason is that employees have complained about a health and safety matter, or if they leave the workplace in circumstances which they reasonably believe to be imminently dangerous.

Statutory rights

Dismissal or selection for redundancy will be automatically unfair if the reason is that an employee is asserting a statutory employment right, eg submitting a case to an Industrial Tribunal, regardless of the employee's length of service or hours of work.

Compensation

If you refuse to re-engage or reinstate an employee after a tribunal order, a compensation award may be granted. The upper limit on a compensation award may be exceeded in certain cases where reinstatement or re-engagement orders have not been fully complied with.

Sex discrimination

Employees can challenge at an Industrial Tribunal any terms in a collective agreement or the rules of an employer which apply to them and which contravene the principle of equal treatment. For example, an agreement which said that, in a redundancy situation, part-time workers would be the first to be selected for redundancy, may discriminate against women if most of the part-time workers were women.

If the Tribunal finds the complaint to be well founded it must make an order declaring the term or rule to be void.

Transfer of ownership

Where an undertaking is transferred to a new employer, whether in the public or private sector, employees have a right to have their contracts of employment with the former employer maintained. This can have major implications for private companies seeking to take over services which are contracted out by the public sector.

Redundancy – consultation with recognised trade unions

The Act has also changed the law on consultation with unions over redundancies:

a) The definition of redundancy, for consultation purposes, has been widened.

b) Compensation awarded against employers for failure to consult properly, can no longer be offset against pay or pay in-lieu of notice.

c) Employers must consult with a view to reaching agreement.

d) Trade unions must be given details of the calculation of redundancy pay. The statutory redundancy payments system has not changed.

Trade unions and industrial action

Membership

a) Employees are free to join any trade union they wish, except where membership is limited to particular occupations or skills.

b) Individuals cannot be excluded for inter-union agreements, and you cannot expel anyone unfairly. It is unlawful to penalise an employee due to their trade union membership.

c) If you unlawfully exclude or expel an employee, they can complain to an Industrial Tribunal.

d) You are only allowed to deduct membership dues with the employee's written permission. This must be renewed every three years or when the rate changes. Trade unions may not expel a member for leaving this system, joining another union or for being a non member.

e) Rules have now become more strict on trade union ballots. Union merger ballots will be subject to independent scrutiny. Trade unions are not allowed to distribute material which may influence voting in a merger ballot.

Industrial action
a) Industrial action ballots must be conducted by postal voting.
b) Seven days notice of the ballot and any industrial action must be given to you by the trade union. You are entitled to the full results of the ballot.
c) Individuals deprived of goods or services due to unlawful industrial action can take legal action. An independent commissioner can be appointed to help the individual exercise this right.

Independent scrutiny
Trade union ballots will be scrutinised more closely, with emphasis on inspecting the membership register and reporting any findings.

Published information
More information will be published by the unions including financial information such as pay and benefits of its leaders and annual written statements. The appointment of a certification officer means that the trade union's financial affairs can be investigated.

Other provisions

i) Wages Councils – Wages Councils have been abolished and there is now no minimum rate of pay.

ii) Industrial Tribunals

   a) Industrial Tribunals can now deal with certain breach of contract cases.

   b) An agreement may be made between an employee and an employer that a settlement be legally binding and prevents the employee going to an Industrial Tribunal provided that the employee has had independent legal advice.

   c) In sexual harassment cases, anonymity can now be given to the parties.

iii) ACAS – The objectives of ACAS have been redefined and charges may be made for some services.

USEFUL TIPS

- *Review your employment procedures and documentation to ensure that you are complying with the law. Ensure any reference material you use is up to date.*

- *Get legal advice if you intend to take action against an employee.*

24 Transfer of Undertakings Regulations 1981

(Protection of Employment)

This section looks at the legislation which provides for the rights of employees when the ownership of a business changes.

Introduction

TUPE was introduced in response to a European Commission Directive. The Regulations aim to prevent employees losing rights, benefits, or their jobs, when a change of employer occurs through transfer of a business.

A business (or undertaking) may transfer from one owner to another by sale or on the owner's death. The business can be a sole trader, a company, or a partnership. The change of ownership can be made up of a series of two or more transfers. A change of ownership because of share transfer is not covered by TUPE because the employer (the Company) remains the same. The Trade Union Reform and Employment Rights Act 1993 (TURER) extended the Regulations to include non-commercial undertakings. The Regulations do not affect employment rights existing under previous laws or regulations.

Who is affected by TUPE?

All employees in a transferred business are covered by the Regulations. The previous employer and the new employer need to know their responsibilities under TUPE.

The Regulations allow scope for necessary redundancies if discussions are initiated, alternatives considered, and there are what the Regulations and a tribunal sees as reasonable circumstances. It is vital that employers considering a transfer understand the implications: claims for unfair dismissal, complaints to tribunals, employee uncertainty and resulting poor publicity can damage a business.

The terms of the Regulations

When a business changes hands all the employees become employees of the new owner, with unchanged contract terms and conditions. This does not include occupational pension rights. (There is protection for occupational pension rights earned up to transfer contained in social security legislation and pension trust arrangements.) Employees' continuity of service is unaffected. The new employer does not take on criminal liabilities.

A new employer cannot make conditions of employment worse without agreement.

Employees taken on just before transfer automatically transfer to the new employer, unless they refuse, in which case their contract is terminated without dismissal. Employees may not be dismissed as a result of the transfer, unless certain criteria are fulfilled. They can complain to a tribunal if they feel they have been unfairly dismissed.

If there is a fundamental change in the terms and conditions of employment (and certain criteria are not fulfilled) employees can terminate their contracts and claim unfair dismissal. Having a new employer is not by itself a ground for claiming unfair dismissal.

The date an employee started (with the previous employer) should be written in their conditions and terms of employment.

Any agreements (including contracts of employment) are invalid if they exclude or limit employees' rights under the Regulations.

If an independent trade union is recognised, union representatives have the right to be informed by the old and new employer about the transfer, and to be consulted about further measures regarding affected employees. Union recognition and agreements in force at the date of transfer are taken over by the new employer.

TURER applied various changes to transfers on/after 30 August 1993, and clarified other aspects of the original Regulations:

i) The Regulations now apply to non-commercial undertakings.

ii) Complete ownership is not strictly necessary — it is possible to transfer franchises, leases, etc.

iii) Consultation between employee representatives and the employer must aim to reach agreement, and if dismissals are considered, attempts to limit or avoid them, or the circumstances which make them necessary, must be discussed with union representatives.

iv) If there is no consultation between employer and employee representative, a tribunal may order compensation of up to four weeks pay for employees (previously two weeks), which under TURER cannot be offset against wages in lieu of notice.

v) Employees do not have to agree to transfer to the new employer, in which case their contracts can be terminated without dismissal.

Situations in which TUPE applies

The Regulations apply to both public and private companies, very large and very small firms. They cover:

i) Transfer of a whole or part business, ie the whole business does not need to be transferred for regulations to apply.

ii) Two businesses merging to form one.

iii) Transfer of a contract for services or goods which acts as a transfer of a business to a new employer.

iv) Sale and transfer of all or part of a sole trader's business, or a partnership.

v) Where a company buys part of or all of a company, and buys the assets and runs the business, rather than just buying shares.

Situations in which TUPE does not apply

i) Transfers outside the UK.

ii) Situations where only assets are bought (and therefore transferred).

iii) Where there is a transfer of contract to provide goods or services, but not involving the transfer of a business or part of a business.

iv) When shares are sold, as the company employing people is still the same company.

v) The parts of the Regulations dealing with dismissal, the employer's duty to inform union representatives, etc do not apply to employees whose contracts have them normally working outside the UK.

Trade unions

Union representatives of affected employees (not necessarily employed in the business to be transferred), must be given the following information by the old employer:

i) The reasons for and the date of the transfer.

ii) The legal, economic and social implications of the transfer for employees who will be affected by it.

iii) Any measures in connection with the transfer which will affect employees.

iv) Any measures the new employer is likely to take which will affect the employees. (The new employer must provide the old employer with this information, in time for discussion.)

The information must be provided in time for adequate consultation with, and representation to the employer. If any of these representations are rejected, the employer must give reasons for the rejection, before the transfer goes through. An employer who does not comply as far as reasonably practical, can be forced by a tribunal to pay compensation to employees.

If the transferred business keeps a separate identity under the new owner, any recognition of an independent union must be maintained. Collective agreements between the previous owner and a recognised union also carry over. However, if the business or undertaking does not maintain its identity once transferred, but is absorbed or merged into another firm which does not recognise a union, union recognition will have to be re-negotiated.

Redundancy

i) Dismissed employees may be entitled to redundancy payments – such payments are unaffected by an unfair dismissal claim that fails.

ii) In most circumstances, the new employer cannot keep some staff on and not others; cherry picking is not permitted.

iii) Claims for redundancy payments may have to be made to the old and the new employer if it is unclear whether the regulations apply.

Grounds for unfair dismissal

i) Under TUPE, the usual two years employment rule before being able to bring an unfair dismissal claim does not apply.

ii) If transferred employees suffer a worsening of terms and conditions, they can terminate their contracts and claim unfair dismissal. Dismissal is seen as unfair unless the employer can prove they acted reasonably in taking technical, economic or organisational factors as reason enough to worsen conditions. Even if a tribunal decides that such worsening of conditions was fair in the circumstances, the employee may still be entitled to redundancy.

iii) New conditions need to be comparable overall, or employees may have a claim for unfair dismissal.

iv) If an employee is dismissed just before or after a transfer, it is seen as being as a result of the transfer, unless there is another reason (technical, economic or organisational) for changing the workforce. This reason could be tested under normal unfair dismissal rules.

Industrial tribunals and conciliation

Various groups may be able to complain to a tribunal:

i) Employees who have either been dismissed or have resigned because of the consequences of the transfer. This must be within three months of employment ending (this deadline can be extended in certain circumstances). Some categories of employees are not allowed to claim unfair dismissal.

ii) Trade union representatives when employers do not comply with consultation and information requirements. The complaint must be made within three months of transfer, (this can be extended by the tribunal if it decides that to complain within three months was not reasonably practicable).

iii) Employees who believe they are entitled to a redundancy payout, although this must be applied for within six months of dismissal.

An employer may be the subject of a complaint by a union representative that the employer did not pass on information about a prospective employer's proposed course of action. The employer may claim that it was not practicable to pass on such information because the prospective employer did not give him the relevant information at the correct time. In this instance, the old employer must tell the new employer that this reason will be given – the new employer becomes a party to the tribunal proceedings.

Complaints are referred to ACAS, who will attempt a settlement before a tribunal hearing. Complaints in the tribunal may be upheld against the old or new employer. They may order the employee to be re-instated, and/or order compensation. This could be up to four weeks pay for each employee. If this money is not forthcoming the employees can individually complain to the tribunal within three months of the original award (longer if the tribunal feels it appropriate), which may order payment.

USEFUL TIPS

- *TUPE is subject to change as legal challenges and EC revised drafts alter the regulations; check with a solicitor or the Employment Service.*

- *Keeping employees and their representatives informed at each stage should ease the transfer process.*

- *Even if a complaint is not made to a tribunal, any employee or employer can contact ACAS for a conciliation officer. Information received is confidential and cannot be divulged in a tribunal without permission.*

- *ACAS can also assist with queries as to the scope of the Regulations.*

Appendices

part.
six

25 Checklist for first time employers

Introduction

Taking on your first employee can be daunting. A range of legislation safeguards employee rights, including health, safety and welfare; these must be studied and absorbed. Taxation and National Insurance arrangements must be organised. New management and administration systems must be put into place. Above all, the employer must learn how to manage. Employers who plan ahead, and obtain the appropriate professional support and training, are more likely to succeed when they start to expand their workforce.

Planning

Draw up

a) A job description: job title, job purpose, duties and main responsibilities, hours, etc.

b) A person specification: qualifications and experience, skills, interests, motivation, special circumstances such as any transport they need, and hours they must be available – do you need a full or part-timer, or even a temporary worker?

ii) Cost out a competitive salary level and any additional incentives. Remember to add in your NI contributions for them, etc.

iii) Prepare a statement of terms and conditions of employment if you require any special contractual arrangements.

Recruitment

This is an important stage; make full use of information available. Be fair; discrimination is illegal at all stages.

i) Advertise – to give yourself the widest choice of applicant, advertise widely and use systematic selection methods. Ask all candidates for the same information, so that comparisons are fair.

ii) Interview – stick to the job description, but remember that equally important in a small business is personality and compatibility. If candidates are expected to have particular skills, eg typing, consider arranging a suitable test. Let the candidate know in advance that a test will be held.

iii) Selection – do not discriminate on race, sex or pay. There is extensive legislation designed to prevent discrimination. This includes the Sex Discrimination Act 1975 as amended, the Race Relations Act 1976, and the Equal Pay Act 1970 as amended. Only in very rare circumstances, where there is a Genuine Occupational Qualification (GOQ), is positive discrimination allowed. In case there are complaints from rejected candidates, retain documentation on applicants and interviews for a short period, eg six months.

Appointment

At this point the importance of legislation takes over from recruitment guidelines.

i) Usually a job offer is spoken, then made in writing. Both methods constitute a contract; if you break this the individual can claim damages. You may decide a three month probationary period is appropriate.

ii) Inform unsuccessful candidates; try to supply a simple letter explaining the reasons why they were unsuccessful, eg that the standard was high, but further experience won.

iii) Provide the successful applicant with a written statement of terms and conditions of employment. Legally, this must be done within two months of starting work. This can be done in stages, but there must be a single 'principal statement' which covers:
   a) Name of employee and employer

b) Dates of start of employment and of continuous employment

c) Rate of pay and pay intervals (hourly, weekly, monthly)

d) Specific terms and conditions on hours of work, holiday pay and entitlement

e) Job title/description

f) Place of work.

The other information should cover:

i) Terms and conditions concerning sickness;

ii) Pension scheme details if applicable

ii) Length of notice required by each side

iv) End date of fixed contracts

v) Details of any collective agreements

vi) Details of conditions relating to work outside the country

vii) Details of how to pursue a grievance.

Induction and training

Plan a thorough induction programme

Spending time on this will save time and problems later. However, at the same time overloading the new employee with information on the first day can make the job seem far more daunting than is necessary. When you have established your programme and see that it works, write it down as a policy for when you next take someone on (section thirteen).

Assess training needs regularly

Training required may be informal (eg meetings); formal on-the-job training; or external training paid for by the business. Contact your local Training and Enterprise Council (TEC), or Local Enterprise Company (LEC) in Scotland, who can assist with training. There may also be grants available.

Budget for training

See this as a continuing investment in the business. If you skimp on this the business may suffer from under-trained and under-qualified staff.

Pay As You Earn (PAYE) and National Insurance (NI)

i) Before your employee starts work, contact your local tax office to arrange PAYE (for collection of income tax) and NI. It is very important that you get this right; if income tax and NI are not deducted then it is the employer who is liable, not the employee. You will be sent:

   a) Deductions working sheets (P11) for income tax and NI.

- b) Tax codes, tables and directions for use.
- c) NI 'Not Contracted-Out Contributions Tables CA38' (CF 391).
- d) NI 'Contributions Manual for Employers CA28' (NI 269).

    Whilst at first sight, calculation of tax and NI looks complicated, it is in fact straightforward. The tax office will provide full and clear instructions.

ii) Ask the new employee to bring on the first day their National Insurance (NI) number, P45 and bank details if you will be crediting salary direct to a bank account.

iii) PAYE – When your employee starts work, you must fill in one of the following documents:

- a) P45 – if the new employee has come from another job or has been claiming unemployment benefit, they should bring Parts 2 and 3 of this document with them; you should follow the instructions on Part 2, and send Part 3 to the tax office straight away.
- b) P46 – some new employees may not have a P45; they may not have worked before, or this may be a second job. If this is the case, and the

employee is paid more than £66.50 per week and works for more than one week, then a P46 should be filled out.

iv) NI – your and their contributions must be recorded on the working deductions sheet P11.

    a) There are no NI contributions from employer or employees if the employees earn less than the Lower Earnings Limit (LEL), which for the tax year 1997-98 is £62 per year; or for those under 16 on pay-day.

    b) The Class 1 rates for employers currently range from 3% to 10.2% of all earnings of employees; although there is an upper limit for employee contributions, there is no such limit for employers.

v) Records

    a) If the employee is to be paid less than the PAYE threshold, do not send their P46 to the tax office; fill in the reverse and retain it for at least three years after the end of the tax year.

    b) If your average NI and PAYE liabilities are not more than £600 per month, you can pay quarterly. Otherwise the tax and NI deducted must be paid to the Collector of Taxes within 14 days of the end of the income tax month, which always ends on the fifth.

c) At the end of the tax year fill in Form 35 (the Employer's Annual Declaration and Certificate) and send it to the Collector of Taxes, along with relevant forms for each employee. You should also give employees Form P60.

Other financial arrangements

i) Obtain Employer's Liability Insurance. This should be obtained through an insurance broker, and must by law have a minimum of £2 million cover. Most policies insure for £10 million.

ii) Prepare itemised pay statements to be given to employees on or before pay day.

Health and safety

Firms with fewer than five employees do not have to prepare a written statement on health and safety policy. However there are other aspects which must be considered.

i) Assessment of the risks in the workplace. Under the Management of Health and Safety at Work Regulations 1992 employers must undertake an assessment of risk to the health and safety of employees and those who may be affected by their employees in the course of their work. Through this, corrective and protective measures which allow compliance with statutory provisions can be taken. Depending on your business activity, you may need to obtain training or secure the services of a health and safety consultant.

ii) The Health and Safety at Work Act 1974, and subsequent regulations such as COSHH 1994, impose an obligation on employers to instruct, inform and train employees who may be exposed to hazardous substances or processes at work.

iii) You may need to consult other legislation such as the Health and Safety (Display Screen Equipment) Regulations 1992; the Provision and Use of Work Equipment Regulations 1992; and the Workplace (Health, Safety and Welfare) Regulations 1992.

Management

i) Draw up a personnel policy document. This will help you to think through the issues and will provide a useful point of reference as to your responsibilities.

ii) Consider taking a management skills course. Not only will you have to manage your own time, but someone else's as well. However it is most important to approach management with an open mind, as there are no hard and fast rules. Basic time management skills and a reputation for approachability should be enough until you have learnt more by experience.

iii) Consider giving a formal appraisal. Appraisals are not essential, but are a good idea once you start to employ more than one or two people. They could be held every six months, and possibly after the first three months. Appraisals should not only cover past events and progress, but also a development path for the person.

USEFUL TIPS

- *Consider training in management skills, but remember that people management cannot be learned solely from a book. Accept you will make mistakes and don't expect to be the perfect manager overnight; these probably don't exist anyway.*

- *Make use of appropriate professional advisers (eg accountant, solicitor, health and safety consultant, recruitment agency).*

26 Further reading

Section 1

Practical Manpower Planning, John Bramham, Institute of Personnel Management, 1988

Handbook of Management, Dennis Lock (Ed), Gower, 1995

Manpower Planning, Gareth Stainer, Heinemann, 1971

Section 2

Managing People for the First Time, Peter Stannack, Pitman, 1993

A Handbook of Personnel Management Practice, Michael Armstrong, Kogan Page, 1991

Hiring and Firing, Karen Lanz, Pitman Publishing, 1988

Managing People at Work, John Hunt, McGraw Hill, 1992

Section 3

Managing People for the First Time, Peter Stannack, Pitman, 1993

Employing and Managing People, Karen Lanz, Pitman Publishing, 1991

Personnel in Practice – Records and Procedure, Croner Publications Ltd

Section 4

Recruiting: How to do it, Iain Maitland, Cassell, 1997

A Handbook of Personnel Management Practice, Michael Armstrong, Kogan Page, 1996

Section 6

Interviews: Skills and Strategy, John Courtis, Institute of Personnel Management, 1988

Hiring and Firing, Karen Lanz, Pitman Publishing, 1988

Section 7

A Guide to the Implementation of an Equal Opportunity Policy, Sheena Dunbar and Larry Ward, MIND North East, 1987

Employment Law Handbook, Income Data Services Ltd

Code of Practice, Commission for Racial Equality

Section 8

Croner's Reference Book for the Self Employed and Smaller Business, Croner Publications Ltd

Employing and Managing People, Karen Lanz, Pitman Publishing, 1991

Maternity Rights – A Guide for Employers and Employees, Department of Trade and Industry, 1995

Sections 9 and 10

A Brief Guide to the DDA DL40

Disability Discrimination Act Information Pack DL50

DDA 1995 – What Service Providers Need to Know DL150

DDA 1995 – What Employers Need to Know DL170, Disability on the Agenda

Sources of Information and Advice PGP6, The Employment Service

The Code of Practice for the Elimination of Discrimination in the Field of Employment

Guidance on Matters to be taken into Account in Determining Questions relating to the Definition of Disability, HMSO

DDA Factsheets, Royal National Institute for the Blind

Section 11

The Trade Union Reform and Employment Rights Act 1993, HMSO

The Law of Employment: A Practical Guide, Paul Lewis, Kogan Page, 1995

Tolley's Drafting Contract of Employment, G Howard, Tolley, 1990

Section 12

Personnel in Practice: Records and Procedures, Croner Publications Ltd

Croner's Reference Book for the Self Employed and Small Business, Croner Publications Ltd

Section 13

Successful Induction, Judy Skeats, Kogan Page, 1996

Employing and managing people,
Karen Lanz, Pitman Publishing, 1991

Section 14

How to Set up and Run an Effective Job Evaluation and Remuneration System, Frans Poels, Kogan Page, 1997

Reward Management, M Armstrong and H Murlis, Kogan Page, 1994

Section 15

Attacking Absenteeism, L.Tylczak, Kogan Page, 1991

Managing Employee Absenteeism, S.Rhodes and R.Steers, Addison Wesley, 1990

Absence (Advisory Booklet 5), ACAS, 1985

Section 16

Croner's Personnel in Practice – Records and Procedures, Croner Publications Ltd

Croner's Guide to Managing Absence, Croner Publications Ltd

Employment Legislation Booklet Series,
Employment Department:

Employing and Managing People,
Karen Lanz, Pitman, 1991

The Handbook of Communication Skills,
Bernice Hurst, Kogan Page, 1991

Constructive Conflict Management,
John Crawley, Nicholas Brealey Publishing Ltd, 1992

Employment Relations,
Hartley and Stephenson (editors),
Blackwell Publishers, 1992

Section 17

Appraisal and Appraisal Interviewing,
Ian Lawson, Industrial Society Press

The Skills of Appraisal,
P Packard & J Slater, Gower, 1987

Section 19

Employment Law (11th edition),
Christopher Waud, Kogan Page, 1995

Dismissal Law (2nd edition),
Martin Edwards, Kogan Page, 1993

Termination of Employment,
Robert Upex, Sweet & Maxwell, 1991

Employing and Managing People,
Karen Lanz, Pitman, 1991

Section 20

The range of Employment Department leaflets, available from your local Employment Service Job Centre includes several which may be useful as follows:

PL 756	*Procedures for Handling Redundancy*
PL 808	*Redundancy Payments*
PL 827	*Limits on Payments*
PL 833	*Redundancy Consultation and Notification*
PL 711	*Rules Governing Continuous Employment and a Weeks Pay*
PL 699	*Employment Rights on the Transfer of an Undertaking*
PL 718	*Employee's Rights on Insolvency of Employer*
PL 707	*Rights to Notice and Reasons for Dismissal*

PL 714   *Fair and Unfair Dismissal*

PL 703   *Facing Redundancy*

All of the above are revised in light of any new legislation, ensure that you obtain the most recent edition.

Employing and Managing People,
Karen Lantz, Pitman, 1991

Law for Small Businesses, Holmes, Evans, Wright and Wright, Pitman, 1991

Section 21

Managing Difficult Staff, Helga Drummoind, Kogan Page, 1980

Sections 22 and 23

The Central Office of Information produce a number of useful leaflets about trade unions and employment legislation for the Department of Employment. You can often pick them up at Job Centres or your local ACAS office.

The Trade Union Reform and Employment Rights Act 1993, HMSO

Croner's Reference Book for the Self-Employed and Smaller Businesses, Croner Publications Ltd

Section 24

The Employment Department publish a series of booklets (available from local Job Centres and Employment Service offices) including:

Employment Rights on the Transfer of an Undertaking PL699

Employing People: a Handbook for Small Firms, ACAS

Croner's Employment Law, Croner Publications Ltd

Gower's Reference Book for the Self-Employed and Smaller Business, Croner Publications Ltd

27 **Useful addresses**

Addresses and telephone numbers for your local **Business Link, Training and Enterprise Council** (**Local Enterprise Company** in Scotland) and **Local Enterprise Agency** may be found in your telephone directory.

The Business Link Signpost service on (0345) 567 765 can put you in touch with your nearest Business Link office, or look on the Internet at http://www.businesslink.co.uk

Local **Scottish Business Shops** can be contacted on (0141) 248 6014 or (0800) 787 878.

For **Business Connect in Wales** call (0345) 969 798.

Local Enterprise Development Unit (LEDU) in Northern Ireland can be contacted on (01232) 491 031.

The National Federation of Enterprise Agencies can put you in touch with your nearest enterprise agency. Ring them on (01234) 354055 or look on the Internet at http://www.pne.org/cobweb/nfea

Livewire helps young people to explore the option of starting or developing their own business. Ring them on (0191) 261 5584 or look on the Internet at http://www.shell-livewire.org

Project North East has set up an Internet site which may be of interest to anyone starting or already in business at http://www.pne.org/cobweb

Addresses for your local Job Centre and Employment Service office can be found in the phone book under 'Employment Service'.

Advisory Conciliation and Arbitration Service (ACAS)
27 Wilton Street
London SW1X 7AZ
Tel: (0171) 210 3613

Equal Opportunities Commission
Overseas House, Quay Street
Manchester M3 3HN
Tel: (0161) 833 9244

Commission for Racial Equality
Yorkshire Bank Chambers
1st Floor, Infirmary Street
Leeds LS1 2JP
Tel: (0113) 243 4413

Race Relations Employment Advisory Service
236 Grays Inn Road
London WC1X 8HL
Tel: (0171) 211 4566
(also regional offices)

Opportunities for People with Disabilities
1 Bank Buildings
Princes Street
London EC2R 8EU
Tel: (0171) 726 4961

The Employment Service (TES) Disability Services Branch
Rockingham House
123 West Street
Sheffield S1 4ER
Tel: (0114) 259 6151

Royal Association for Disability and Rehabilitation (RADAR)
Unit 12, City Forum
250 City Road
London EC1V 8AF
Tel: (0171) 250 3222

National Disabilities Council
The Adelphi, 1-11 John Adam Street
London WC2N 6HT
Tel: (0171) 712 2099

**Royal National Institute
for the Blind (RNIB)**
224 Great Portland Street
London W1N 6AA
Tel: (0171) 388 1266

Employers' Forum on Disability
Nutmeg House, 60 Gainsford Street
London SE1 2NY
Tel: (0171) 403 3020

Confederation of British Industry
Centre Point, 103 New Oxford Street
London WC1A 1DU
Tel: (0171) 379 7400

Trades Union Congress (TUC)
Congress House
Great Russell Street
London WC1B 3LS
Tel: (0171) 636 4030

The Industrial Society
Small Business Department
Robert Hyde House
48 Bryanston Square
London W1H 7LN
Tel: (0171) 262 2401

Institute of Personnel and Development
35 Camp Road, London SW19 4UX
Tel: (0181) 946 9100

Central Offices of the Industrial Tribunals:

England and Wales
19-29 Woburn Place, Russell Square
London WC1H 0LU
Tel: (0171) 273 3000

Scotland
Franborough House
123-157 Bothwell Street
Glasgow G2 7JR
Tel: (0141) 204 2677

Northern Ireland
20-24 Waring Street
Belfast BT1 2EB
Tel: (01232) 327 666

Certification Officer for Trade Unions and Employers' Associations
Brandon House
180 Borough High Street
London SE1 1LW
Tel: (0171) 210 3735

Health and Safety Information Centres, HSE
Baynards House, 1 Chepstow Place
Westbourne Place
London W2 4TF
Tel: (0171) 221 0870

Index

Absence	171
Advertising	61
Appraisal	193
Closed shop agreements	184, 249
Collective bargaining	165
Communication	186
Conditions of employment	133
Conflict	235
Contract of employment	131, 144
Disability discrimination	85, 107
Disability Discrimination Act	117
Discipline	203
Discrimination	55, 69
Dismissal	174, 210, 215
Employee relations	181
Equal opportunities	85
Equal pay	85
Genuine Occupational Qualification	87
Grievance procedure	92
Hawthorne Electric Co	13
Health and safety	249

Health and safety policy	147, 148
Herzberg, Frederick	5
Hierarchy of needs	3
Hygiene factors	5
Induction checklists	155, 282
Industrial action	250
Industrial relations	181
Interviewing	73
Job description	30, 41
Maslow, Abraham	3
Maternity rights	95
Mayo, Elton	13
McGregor, Douglas	6
Motivators	5
Negotiation	188
Notice periods	222
Participation	13
Pay	9, 161
Person specification	30, 51
Personnel policy statements	141
Planning	
Praise	11
Profit related pay	168

Quality circles	14
Race discrimination	85
Recruitment	29
Redundancy	225, 271
Restraint of trade	139
Sex discrimination	85
Share option schemes	168
Sickness	171
Staff development	25, 199
Staff handbook	148, 157
Staff induction	151
Staff planning	19
Statement of terms and conditions of employment	134
Statutory Maternity Pay	101
Statutory sick pay	176
Targets	15
Task analysis	30
Theory X and Y	6
Trade unions	183, 247
Transfer of Undertakings	265
TURER	255
Unfair dismissal	219
Work design	12

Hawksmere – focused on helping you improve your performance

Hawksmere plc is one of the UK's foremost training organisations. We design and present more than 450 public seminars a year, in the UK and internationally, for professionals and executives in business, industry and the public sector, in addition to a comprehensive programme of specially tailored in-company courses. Every year, well over 15,000 people attend a Hawksmere programme. The companies which use our programmes and the number of courses we successfully repeat reflect our reputation for uncompromising quality.

Our policy is to continually re-examine and develop our programmes, updating and improving them. Our aim is to anticipate the shifting and often complex challenges facing everyone in business and the professions and to provide programmes of high quality, focused on producing practical results – helping you improve your performance.

Our objective for each delegate

At Hawksmere we have one major aim – that every delegate leaves each programme better equipped to put enhanced techniques and expertise to practical use. All our speakers are practitioners who are experts in their own field: as a result, the information and advice on offer at a Hawksmere programme is expert and tried and tested, practical yet up-to-the-minute.

Our programmes span all levels, from introductory skills to sophisticated techniques and the implications of complex legislation. Reflecting their different aims and objectives, they also vary in format from one day multi-speaker conferences to one and two day seminars, three day courses and week long residential workshops.

For a brochure on any particular area of interest or for more information generally, please call Hawksmere Customer Services on 0171 824 8257 or fax on 0171 730 4293.

Hawksmere In-company Training

In addition to its public seminars Hawksmere works with client companies developing and delivering a wide range of tailored training in industries as diverse as retailing, pharmaceuticals, public relations, engineering and service industries such as banking and insurance – the list is long.

We specialise in a wide range of personnel topics including Personnel and Employment Law, Competencies, Empowerment, Coaching, Appraisal, Interviewing, Communication and Motivation.

The Hawksmere In-Company team is headed by Aileen Clark, who has worked extensively in management training and development for the past twenty years, building successful courses for a wide range of businesses in both the public and private sectors. Call Aileen or her team on 0171 824 8257 for expert advice on your training needs without any obligation.

Thorogood: the publishing business of the Hawksmere Group

Thorogood publishes a wide range of books, reports, special briefings, psychometric tests and videos.

Listed below is a selection of key titles.

Masters in Management

Mastering business planning and strategy *Paul Elkin*	£19.95
Mastering financial management *Stephen Brookson*	£19.95
Mastering leadership *Michael Williams*	£19.95
Mastering negotiations *Eric Evans*	£19.95
Mastering people management *Mark Thomas*	£19.95
Mastering project management *Cathy Lake*	£19.95

The Essential Guides

The essential guide to buying
and selling unquoted businesses
Ian Smith £25

The essential guide to business
planning and raising finance
Naomi Langford-Wood & Brian Salter £25

The essential business guide to the Internet
Naomi Langford-Wood & Brian Salter £19.95

Other titles

The John Adair handbook of management
and leadership – *edited by Neil Thomas*
£19.95

The handbook of management fads
Steve Morris £8.95

The inside track to successful management
Dr Gerald Kushel £16.95

The pension trustee's handbook (2nd edition)
Robin Ellison £25

Reports and Special Briefings

Dynamic budgetary control
David Allen £95

Evaluating and monitoring strategies
David Allen £95

Software licence agreements
Robert Bond £125

Negotiation tactics for software and hi-tech
agreements – *Robert Bond* £165

Achieving business excellence, quality and
performance improvement
Colin Chapman and Dennis Hopper £95

Employment law aspects of mergers
and acquisitions – *Michael Ryley* £125

Techniques for successful
management buy-outs – *Ian Smith* £125

Financial techniques for business
acquisitions and disposals – *Ian Smith* £125

Techniques for minimising the risks of
acquisitions: commercial due diligence
Ian Smith & Kevin Jewell £125

Mergers and acquisitions – confronting
the organisation and people issue
Mark Thomas £125

An employer's guide to the management of
complaints of sex and race discrimination
Christopher Walter £125

Securing business funding from
Europe and the UK – *Peter Wilding* £125

Influencing the European Union
Peter Wilding £125

Standard conditions of commercial contract
Peter Wilding £139

To order any title, or to request more information, please call Thorogood Customer Services on 0171 824 8257 or fax on 0171 730 4293.